Celebrities Are Groupies Too!

Celebrities Are Groupies Too!

Donna Mary Andujar

Lived by China Starr, written by Peavy

iUniverse, Inc.
New York Lincoln Shanghai

Celebrities Are Groupies Too!

Copyright © 2008 by DONNA ANDUJAR

All rights reserved. No part of this book may be used or reproduced by any means, graphic, electronic, or mechanical, including photocopying, recording, taping or by any information storage retrieval system without the written permission of the publisher except in the case of brief quotations embodied in critical articles and reviews.

iUniverse books may be ordered through booksellers or by contacting:

iUniverse
2021 Pine Lake Road, Suite 100
Lincoln, NE 68512
www.iuniverse.com
1-800-Authors (1-800-288-4677)

Because of the dynamic nature of the Internet, any Web addresses or links contained in this book may have changed since publication and may no longer be valid.

The views expressed in this work are solely those of the author and do not necessarily reflect the views of the publisher, and the publisher hereby disclaims any responsibility for them.

ISBN: 978-0-595-47845-3 (pbk)
ISBN: 978-0-595-60042-7 (ebk)

Printed in the United States of America

I'd like to dedicate this book to all the women across the world who have been victims of domestic violence, abuse, rape and abandonment ... who never thought they could get help and make it out of their situations and make a better life for themselves. This one's for you.

China Starr'S

Contents

Acknowledgements ix
CHAPTER 1	Survival of The Fittest 1
CHAPTER 2	Beauty & Da NY Beasts 8
CHAPTER 3	From Ashy to Classy 15
CHAPTER 4	Eating My Cake 22
CHAPTER 5	Back On My Grind 28
CHAPTER 6	Waking Up To Reality 40
CHAPTER 7	Vacation Time 48
CHAPTER 8	Checked Into Heaven 52
CHAPTER 9	Free To Do Me 58
CHAPTER 10	When One Door Closes Another Opens 65
CHAPTER 11	Overnight Celebrity 75
CHAPTER 12	The Pros and The Cons 82
CHAPTER 13	"The Prelude" 88

Acknowledgements

To God-Without you nothing wouldn't be possible. You gave me the strength to over come all of these obstacles in my life and give me the strength to move on.

To My Daughter Tatiana-You give me a new meaning to life, because of you I have found it more important for me to succeed and I hope that when you read this you will learn from my mistakes in life, because, "Nobody is perfect." I pray that GOD keeps you away from harm and that you achieve all that you desire in life.

To My Mom-Thanks for sticking it out with five kids and even though you made dire mistakes in raising us, I give you credit for whatever you was able to provide for us. You're always in my prayers.

To My Two Sisters: Chasity and Yvette-Thanx Chaz for supporting me concerning this book, and to Yvette, I hope one day you will learn that you have to love yourself even when people don't love you as much. I'm glad that although late in my life we were able to meet up and hang out and catch up on each other's life. I wish you guys would have been there more for me throughout my life, but "What didn't kill me made me stronger."

To Shawn-I'm sorry because of all that you put me through, I have learned to forgive you but I will never forget what you did to me. All I can do is pray for you. Yes you helped me out financially throughout my early adulthood, but AT what cost? I'm glad I learned early that money isn't everything in life, and that my life was more important then clothes, furniture and everything else I lost when I had to go to the shelter with OUR four year old daughter because you felt you were right for hitting me. There's never a good enough excuse.

Thanx to Ray Daniels CEO of Drahma Magazine for promoting my book for me and giving me a chance to tell my story, you can always stand under my umbrella. I wish you good luck in all your dreams and good things come to good people.

To Peavy-Thanks for helping me write my book, you're a great ghostwriter. You put your twist and jokes into the story to make it sound more funnier, and helped me write my book to it's full potential. Good luck on your books you have out, "The Reparation" and "A Classic."

Thanx to Wendy Williams for opening doors for me, you didn't have to bring me on the show. You are truly the "Queen of This Radio Shit" and drahma! And yes every great has copycats and you know who you hating ass bitches are. There's no need for me to mention your name cause when I said it you already thought about it yourself! You do make room for people in this industry and I am a prime example of that. You're not a hater, you look comfortable in your own skin and are definitely a role model to me.

Miss Jones thanx to you too for helping me promote my book, my mamma always told me, "When they stop talking about you-you better worry" and she was right! Thanx for also having the balls to allow me on your show, even when you knew that Funk Master Flex was in my book, and to Michael Sean and Envy as well, keep promoting me thanx! LOL. Let me stop, I wouldn't WANT Funk Master Flex to get yah fired, lol. Oh' yea, when ya'll stop snitching on celeb's then I'll stop.

To Suige, Ms. Envy, Vaughn from allthaclubz.com, Kurt Flirt from datzwhatzup.net, Hood Promo, Rober Southoff, all my fans from my college-Touro College, Weeksville Projects, my best friend Ebony Davidson, Necee, Kema, Poche Girl, all my haters "Do your job!", Alissa, The Dr. Keith Ablow Show, Fox 5, Mc Serch, Mel Matrix, my cousin Tatiana Madina, Swet Magazine, all my MYSPACE FRIENDS @ myspace.com/brooklynchina, King Dome, Craig G, "SPliff Star" MY "HOMMIE" and every and anybody that I missed, thanx for supporting me on this book and keeping me focused, God bless all of yah, China Starr Muahz! ;~)

1

Survival of The Fittest

I was born in Kings County Hospital in Brooklyn, NY and from the beginning it was painfully obvious life for China Starr was going to be far from sweet or easy to digest. Shit, after you finish this I'm sure you'd ask who'd even want a bite? Without a doubt everything I got I had to fight for with the exception of the hand me downs I was forced to wear, which in actually was the least of the shit I had to worry about being the third born of five children raised by a single mother on welfare in a cramped ass apartment in the middle of Do or Die Bedstuy. Trust and believe there were more days then I care to remember I was forced to eat cereal with powdered milk for dinner-fuck breakfast, listen when you don't know where your next meal is coming from you'll take whatever you can get when you can get it. Beggars can't be choosey or neither can the truly hungry. Luckily for me there was a church right up the block from where I stayed that would hit me with food every here and there whenever they could. I guess they felt sorry for me or whatever cause I was so young, I don't know, but whatever the reason was I'm glad they did-because sometimes it was the only time I ate. And would you believe with all that I had to go through to get some food, I still had to argue with my sisters to cook the damn shit, I thought if I got us something to eat for that day the least they could do is cook it! I mean if I were able to do it, I would've done it myself and said fuck them. What else could I have possibly done?

I tell you there was never anyone I could actually depend on, Chasity and Yvette were constantly busy in love and doing them and my moms just didn't give a fuck. I don't think she didn't love me, I just think she was tired and worn out from all the shit they put her through when they were younger and by time I came around she just let me run wild and do whatever the fuck I wanted to do, and I did. At one point I just basically became a babysitter for my younger brother Luis when he popped up around "94" which allowed my moms more freedom. She had more then enough free time if you ask me cause I swear my moms would leave us alone for hours at a time in that empty dirty ass apartment to starve. I bullshit you not our apartment was so fucking empty when you walked or talked in our spot you could hear an echo throughout the whole damn house! Literally it was nothing but space, mice and roaches and nothing else, no TV-no nothing, just space.

I remember a bunch of times singing to myself "I'm Going Down" by Mary J Blige and anything else I could think of by Aaliyah to pass time and if I wasn't singing I was guaranteed to be rapping or dancing. I had nothing else to do, I did it so much I became better then most and sooner or later the whole world will see how good I am, I'm telling you I'm hot. I'll show 'em how to really bring Hollywood to the hood, none of that song and dance bullshit they be rocking. It was basically either I entertained myself or went crazy, dead silence will kill you regardless of who you are; you go try staring at bare walls all day and see what the fuck it gets you. Ya ass be in a straight jacket some where in a mental institution talking to birds and yourself and looking into the sky, try it and see, why you think niggas in jail be dreading the hole? Actually the time I spent in that apartment was like living in a cell, living in Brooklyn itself is like being in a jail. Even if you're a kid you're always fighting and looking over your shoulder like any other person would, nobody in Brooklyn gets a break that's why we're New York's toughest and most thorough borough.

It was only every so often my moms would come by and hit us off with a few food stamps for some grub, and even then she'd slide them under the door and bounce and keep it moving or whatever like it was nothing … like it was normal or it wasn't even her own kids on the other side of the door. It all popped off when this racist British mother fucker my mother let live with us for some reason had the nerves to pick me up by the neck and choke the shit out of me, I was only seven and even if I was grown-so what! What right does he have to hit a woman let alone a little girl, I couldn't believe my moms just stood there and watched him! She actually watched him do that shit. The only reason he let me go or I should say I got loose, was because I fucking kicked him in the balls as hard as I could, I was trying to kill his faggot ass for real! I swear I still get heated every time I think about that shit. If I see him today word to everything I love I'd fuck him up just based off the memories of the shit he did, it was bad enough he beat my moms in front of us but damn you wanna fuck up a little girl too? I hope somebody fucks him in the ass and makes him bleed until he can't walk like the little bitch he is. You can say whatever you want but it is what it is, real talk. He used to say to my mother all the time, "I can't live in a house with a bunch of niggers" and I guess he got tired of it so his punk ass eventually left and you know who followed.

I can't believe she gave up everything for him ... even her pride, she took it so far she started to act "white" just to please him. First of all, there is no pleasing a person like that, no matter what you do-you can't, they're miserable and all they want is to see you suffer with them. I'm telling you-you can't. Misery loves company and you know the rest, old folks don't say shit just to say it-believe it, it's been said for a reason, if it weren't the truth it would've died a long time ago. My moms wasn't always like that though, it was only when she was in a relationship with a man that she acted that way. If she was single we was good, far as how she treated us but if a man were involved, you can forget about it-it was a wrap.

I'd say I must've been about eight when my moms decided to send me off to my dads crib to live, which was just the beginning of many years of a cycle of traveling back and forth from Brooklyn to Rochester and vice versa. It was back in Brooklyn I started to develop physically and I aint gotta tell you ... you should already know, I drove my moms crazy. I'm telling you at fourteen my body was banging and I was easily passing for legal although I was really jail bait as they say, I was pretty much getting into any club I wanted like it was nothing. With the rapid maturity of my body I began living an adult's life fast and early, and of course as a child I loved every minute of it.

One night me and my sister Chasity was hanging out at this club called The Melting Pot when I ran into this Philippine dude named Ace who was nineteen back then, at the time that we meet he was a solid five years older then me and he knew it, he just didn't care. Ace had his own apartment somewhere in Manhattan in the hundred blocks of Amsterdam so I was constantly hanging out with him over there, cause I sure as hell wasn't trying to stay home and baby sit. Without saying after a few months of us kicking it and always being around each other we became close and started having sex on a regular basis. We liked each other but overall we were basically just fuck buddies, we'd fuck each other for hours at a time, that's all we did when we were together-we were both young so that's what we did. Common sense will tell you my home life was still fucked up and after awhile since I had another place to stay I said fuck it and left. I was tired of all the shit I was going through living with my moms and she acted like she really didn't care and things weren't getting any better, they just got worse so I figured why should I stay, why not leave? So that's exactly what I did, I didn't even think twice and she still didn't give a fuck!

Living with Ace was nothing luxurious but it was way better then what I had in Brooklyn, even though we stayed together I spent more time by myself then ever. Ace would be going back and forth to work to do whatever he had to do to pay the bills and support us. He never had the greatest jobs or made that much money but he did the best he could, while Ace was out working and taking care of business I would go roller blade in Central Park. I liked spending time in the park but mainly the reason I was always there was to keep myself occupied and kill time until Ace got off and we were back to fucking all night. Our little program worked for the both of us and everything was smooth until he couldn't afford me and I began to lose weight and dress like a whore. I didn't look like myself at all between the combination of the cheap tight clothes he always bought me and all the weight I lost from rarely eating and remaining highly active. I couldn't take the way I looked or was living anymore so by the end of the summer I finally broke down and decided to go home.

I never actually thought I'd see the day that Bedstuy would be where I preferred to be-well at least living in that apartment anyway, actually I didn't really prefer it ... I had no choice. If I had other options, trust me I would've never gone back, I would have stayed somewhere else as long as I could. I was surprised, when I came home I expected my moms to wild out and kick my ass or something but she didn't, she was just glad I was alive because she hadn't seen or heard from me the whole summer. I didn't think I needed to contact her or let her know where I was at or what I was doing in the first place because she didn't seem that interested in what I did anyway when I was there, so why waste my time-you feel me?

Back then and especially around that time I thought I was grown, while I was fucking Ace and living on my own I felt like I was a woman and not just a fourteen year old. Now that I'm really a woman when I look back at it, I was just a helpless child who needed love and direction. Maybe if my moms or any one of my sisters would have stopped me and told me what I really needed to hear, I probably wouldn't have done what I did. It's not my fault nobody took the time to care about me, no it's not all their fault neither but I was a kid and they knew better, they should've done something to help me ... or at least tried. They just sat back and watched me make mistake after mistake like that makes any sense, what's the point of having a family, for all that I could've just been an orphan.

Well anyway soon after I returned home I wouldn't stay there too much longer because I was headed out to Rochester to stay with my dad. I knew my moms could barely afford me more then Ace and my dad could afford me more then either one of them so I went to stay with him. I didn't really want to go upstate but I wasn't trying to walk around looking like a cracked out whore neither, it's unbelievable the choices I had to make. By time I got to Rochester this time around I was far from a child, I completely lost all my innocence and my days of fun and games where gone-if there ever where any. Everything in my life at that point was just a matter of living and nothing else. I don't think I ever was a child, children don't have problems or realize they do, your parents can be poor and you'd never know it if you are loved and happy. I wasn't, maybe that's why it seems as if all I could remember is a struggle.

My mother and father had been off and on for years both going through their fair share of ups and downs the same as any couple does, but when my father got strung out on that hard white in the late eighties early nineties it was a wrap-he was too far gone and my mother left and never looked back. I remember one day going to the pool when me and my sisters bumped into my father digging in the garbage for some food! He looked so fucked up, now that I think about it, but he was my father and all I wanted to do was touch him but my sister wouldn't let me. I didn't know what the fuck was going on, I just knew I felt ashamed and embarrassed because I loved my dad and I was happy to see him but everybody kept screaming "no" and wouldn't let me.

After my father got cleaned up and shook his habit he began to live with a lady named Shirley, she was nice and helped him out as much as she could and I think Shw really loved him. Shirley and my father ended up being together for a while and things were going good between them until he started abusing her and ruined it like he always did. I guess something's are harder to shake then others because he did the same thing to my mother but Shirley wasn't trying to go that route and left him before it even got out of hand. I don't blame her because that's probably the best thing to do in that type of situation, it's better to end it before you get stuck in a completely fucked up situation and can't get out and end up having more trouble on your hands then what it's worth. Trust me I know.

If you haven't been paying attention, by now you should know I come from a very dysfunctional and fucked up family where abuse and suffering is common and takes place as often as most people brush their teeth. You can choose your career, you can choose friends and you can choose who you love and how you love them but you can't choose your family or trade them in for another. You're stuck with who you're stuck with; I never had a choice ... I was born into drama.

In Rochester things got a little better, but it wasn't all peaches and cream but at least I finally lucked up and had clean clothes and a stable environment to grow in. My father's income and Rochester's slowed down pace allowed me the opportunity to live as close to being a kid as possible. Even though it was impossible because I was too far-gone and mentality I was nowhere near my age. I'd experienced too much by that point to ever turn back, the hood got me and damn near raised me. Is it any wonder I quickly became a product of my environment and victim of circumstance? You can take anybody male or female out the hood but once the hood sets in, you can forget about it! It's a part of you for life; it's not as serious as some people make it out to be it just molds you different. People who've lived a hard knock life understand where I'm coming from the hood knows exactly what I mean. That's why I'm so jaded to a lot that goes on because I've seen it all, and where I'm from anything can and will and does happen. I am who I am cause of it and nothings going to change it and that's what it is, and if you don't like it fuck it, it's not gonna change me so get over it.

When I was in Franklin High I automatically got a lot of attention or should I say hate being the hot new thick Puerto Rican chick from the city with a fat ass and you know how that go. Hating season was open and I aired them out when necessary but for the most part I kept to myself, and my boyfriend Raymond. Raymond and I dated for about four years or close to it, Raymond and my pops got along pretty well and my father even told me he thought we would end up getting married but what would he know about that?

True he was married to my moms and all that but I think my father was a molester on the low and my mother knew that, that's why she sent my sister Chasity to live with us upstate for a while to keep an eye on me not to long after I first got there. One day Chasity and I were getting ready for school like all girls do, you know in the bathroom, singing and thinking bout what to wear or whatever. Anyway I was chilling in my bra and panties styling my hair in the bathroom like Mickey Mouse cause back then that was my shit, when all of a sudden my dad comes busting in like "sorry" and walks out. I didn't think nothing of it, I just left it at that till Chasity came in crying not too long after he left.

I didn't know what the fuck was going on or why she was crying so I got worried immediately and asked her what happened, instead of saying what happened she turned and asked me, "Do you know what dad just told me?" I had no idea and was confused even more; I didn't know what to expect her to say so I just asked the obvious, "What?" I couldn't believe Chasity said our father told her that he better had left the bathroom before he forgot that I was his daughter! I was like what! I couldn't believe that shit, he never touched me or hit me but he did let me wear skimpy clothing most parents-especially fathers would never let their daughters wear so I'm sure that's how he got his jollies. I get sick thinking about it ... it's disgusting, I can't believe he did that. Who knows what he did when I wasn't there. After that I made it at point not to be home as much as possible, I'd damn near came back when it was time to go to bed. I couldn't even concentrate in school because of the thoughts I would have of him lusting after me, like damn I'm your youngest daughter, what the fuck was I supposed to do. I couldn't even tell my mother.

That was just part of the reason I had to get out of there, after I told Raymond I had to leave because I wanted to be famous and sitting around there wouldn't do it he began to hit me. I couldn't win it was like if it wasn't one form of abuse it was another. No matter where I turned I ended up in a fucked up situation with no one willing to help, damn you'd think someone would feel my pain. All I know is I would watch music videos on BET, MTV, Video Music Box and whoever else was on and say to myself what do these girls got that I don't, I'm prettier and have a bader body then most of them-I can do that shit, I'm gonna do it. I knew in my heart I would never be able to follow my dreams if I stayed up in Rochester. Yes it served its purpose but everything has its time and place and if I did end up staying there, I'd probably still be there wasting my life as we speak.

I needed to be where the action was at so I took my ass right back to Brooklyn and civilization and ran through every one of the boroughs like I owned that bitch. I might've been back in the hood but I was happier and this time around, I was out for the paper and going to get it however I had to!

2

Beauty & Da NY Beasts

So here I am back around the way: seventeen light skin with a pretty face, chinky eyes, small waste and fat ass in the middle of the Stuy and sticking out like a mother fucker and bout to upset to the whole tri-state like never before seen-not even to this day! I was tired of not having anything for myself, anybody's whose ever been broke will tell you, you get tired of that shit fast. I was constantly being made fun of and cracked on about the beat down kicks I rocked and the played out and fucked up clothes I wore. Who in Brooklyn isn't materialistic, more or less the core of New York State is all about what type of clothes you rock, a proper shoe game, hot v's and hot ass jewels. Basically if you aint got none of the above-you're really not saying nothing and if you only got some of it you're on a paper chase to you get it all and that's just part of the New York swagg.

The mentality of people in Rochester was totally different then New Yorkers from the boroughs or even Long Island, I know for a fact the schools were nothing like Brooklyn's! Upstate the schools are way cleaner and the work is harder because they expect more out of you and they actually want you to learn and majority of the teachers care about you in some way. Teachers in the hood don't give a fuck! They aint no better then anybody else, they lie, steal and cheat to get what they want too. Shit, in Rochester when I went to Franklin High we had lockers, gym equipment, books, grass and even a mother fucking swimming pool! In Sarah J Hale on Dean it was nothing but gangs, thugs, hustlers, drugs and fights. Around my way all I heard was whose going half on a blunt and what new strip clubs was opening, nobody mentioned school or jobs in the same sentence-if they ever said it to begin with. Girls my age weren't concerned with finding a guy they liked who was going to treat them right and all that love shit, it was all about what we could get out of a man and that was it. From an early age it was business never personal even then, it's understood that's how we're breed in the concrete jungle.

When I made my brief return to high school all the hoes got back on their job hating, hard-body! Them chicks in Sarah J were sick because of course their simple ass's thought I was after their broke ass boyfriends when I wasn't. What for, most of the guys loved me and the few who didn't instigated shit with their girlfriends to get at me, I could've picked and choose and if I wanted them but I didn't. Back then even though I didn't have a clique I still wasn't scared of shit, I been handling mine. Everybody knew I had a couple of sisters and all that but I always fought my own battles so the only thing they could do was jump me, and yea you know some of them bitches was plotting but it never went down. Them hoes were pussy and aint really want it with me and they all knew it.

There was this one girl I was cool with for about a year until she turned out to be a snake too, that's mainly why I don't fuck with alot of people and when I do they mostly dudes-feel me. One day out of nowhere my home girl at the time just comes out and tells me her step father wants to fuck me and he'll pay me to I do it, I was thinking to myself, "What the fuck, is this bitch serious!" I aint gonna lie I thought about it at first, what you think I didn't? Hell yea I did, I could've used that money but I thought about it … her moms was a nice lady and I aint wanna violate her so I didn't.

I should've though, especially after how her and greezy ass daughter got down, I should've. After that that miserable bitch always found a way to keep me in trouble. Her lying ass started spreading wild lies about me like I told her I wanted to fuck this girl's man! From the beginning I kept it 100-Brooklyn style, so I hollered at the chick and told her straight out, "Yo I aint say that shit" and I took her to old girls crib to air it out and settle it and set the record straight. Do you know she not only lied to my face but her trifling ass mother cosigned the shit and watched as they jumped me! I guess that's the thanks I get for telling her, her loving husband wanted to fuck me and she called me the "home wrecker"? Check ya man. I'm willing to put money on it her daughter and damn loving husband were fucking and sucking each other all day while she was gone and that's the reason her daughter tried to kill herself swallowing all those pills! It's okay, you know I was back at 'em, this time I brought my people with me … me, my mom's, my sister and her boyfriend all went straight up to her door and knocked like surprise mother fucker it's the mailman! Her and her moms were scared as hell to come outside then but they eventually did and when her moms came out she came out with a bat like she built like that! My moms snatched that shit right out her hand and she ran her ass back in the house ASAP and that was that! Yo the way those bitch ass wanna be gangsters ran back in the house was hilarious you hear me!

I felt like now that I was coming of age numerically, it was time for me to step up and be independent and not look to my moms for nothing. I was back around the way and it was only a matter of time I linked up with my ace from back in the day, Ebony better known to some as Daisy. While I was gone Eb got involved in the strip game early and it's was only a matter time before she put me on and I was a problem in the biz! Through Ebony I meet Jacky and from there she introduced me to a skinny pimp by the name of Cincere. Even though Cincere was a pimp, he was always nice to me but then again he was trying to groom me into his bread and butter so why wouldn't he? It only made sense, at the time he wasn't managing a stable, he was just pimping a girl named Tay-Tay. I can't front Cincere worked Tay-Tay hard and got every last dollar out of her by controlling her mind and body! I spent one weekend with them and that was enough, I saw what he did to her and he sure ass hell wasn't going to do that to me, fuck that! What I look like getting money to give it away to a nigga who aint doing shit but giving orders!

Cincere smelled money when it came to me and I saw opportunity when it came to him, he knew a lot of clubs and I was new to the game so I watched and learned, I'd be damn if I ended up getting fucked over and end up broke. I'm telling you Cincere never pimped me once, but he did put me on my first night dancing …

Actually Ebony's friend Jacky told me to go to a bar with them and the "bar" ended up being a strip club called Wiggles, I was sitting there with Cincere watching Tay-Tay dance and get money! I mean Tay-Tay was literally getting easy money, she just shook her ass here and there and collected her doe and that was it. That was all I needed to see, I was hooked on sight, I told Cincere I wanted to get down and he gave me a drink and took me off to a dressing room and next thing you know I was about to pop my cherry.

I was so nervous; when I opened the dressing room door all I saw was ass everywhere! I know it sounds crazy being I know was in a strip club but it still surprised me that nobody seemed to mind, they all acted like it was normal but it was my first time and it caught me off guard. I wasn't ashamed of my body but I did feel awkward, I remember trying to put on my outfit over my clothes, I was totally unprepared-I had on a pink dress with red shoes! I know, I told you I was unprepared I was just thinking about the money. I know those bitches were looking at me like, "she must have something to hide", but the reality of it was I was just not used to a lifestyle that open. I had seen and been through a lot already but this was completely new, I didn't know what I was getting into or what to expect. I remember I was just about dressed and started bending over to lock my shoes when some girl walked over to me and decided she felt like slapping me on my ass! Normally I would've probably confronted her ass, I don't like people putting their hands on me but that particular time I didn't know how to react … that's when I first realized I was in a place where my property was no longer mine anymore and from that point on I would constantly be touched by whoever and whenever they wanted.

Tay-Tay told the girls in the room, "Listen up this is China's first time dancing" and passed me a shot of Hennessy and advised me it would help relax me while I'm on the stage and from then on liquor and stripping went hand and hand for me! I guess that night I really got turned out, cause by time they called my name and I came out I was ready to test this stripper shit out and I was focused. Like I said I always was a dancer whether I was dancing to Michael Jackson when my dad used to pump him in the crib or it was hip-hop, I was always rocking. I was on beat and everyone male and female watched in aw as I mixed my own special blend of soul and sensuality on the stage. I wasn't just taking my clothes off, I knew what I was doing but I swear I never stripped a day in my life. Cincere thought I was bullshitting him when I told him I didn't because he thought I was a pro and kept asking me, "Are you sure you never danced before?" I'm not going to lie, when that girl slapped me on my ass in the dressing room it made me feel so uncomfortable but when those men slapped my ass, I was far from mad because then money followed behind the touching. Stripping didn't make me feel like I was getting played, it made me feel like I was doing the playing and boy did I play! I played my hand well then Cincere and Tay-Tay tried theirs …

After we finished putting in work for the night we were situating the hotel arrangements and payment when those two sneaky mother fucker's tried to play me, talking about the forty dollars I put down on the room was two boo-boo twenties and they needed more money! Yea right, come on I was young but not that fucking young-their game was see through and it only pushed me to move faster. Even though they tried to get me, the whole time I'm around them I kept thinking to myself, "Damn Cincere is a nice guy and all but why the hell is this chick so infatuated with him? She's wrapped around his finger." And then I found out, she wasn't really wrapped around his finger at all-she was wrapped around his dick! That nigga Cincere's dick is hung like a horse! After we finally got our financial issue straight, me, Tay-Tay and Cincere had a threesome … kind of. Cincere kept trying to put his dick in me but it wouldn't work because his shit was way too big so he got mad and complained about how he didn't want no tight pussy so I said fuck it and rolled over and let them go at it. But by the way Tay-Tay was screaming you would've thought that was the first time they fucked and I know he blew her back out on a regular basis. I figured if she couldn't take it, nobody can get used to a dick like that and I knew he sure as hell wasn't gonna be digging in me all damn night with that oversized dick! I been made up my mind and was out, fuck that!

During the time I started stripping I was still in school and living with my moms so I was able to stack a little something. I remember the first day I came home and told my moms I was stripping, I thought she was going to blackout and go at my ass but she just said, "well at least you can pay some bills around here" and left it at that. I think it was kind of, nah it was fucked up she let me strip at seventeen, I was still a decent kid and there was still hope. The main reason I was stripping was cause she couldn't take care of me in the first place, I wasn't doing it just because I like to dance, it was my hustle and I had to. I understand my mother wanted me to learn the hard way but at what cost? The road I was traveling down would eventually lead me into all sorts of things and none that great. Even my sisters took notice of how feed up and tired my moms had become, one day Yvette said to my mother right before she dropped me off to work, "I can't believe you're dropping her off to a strip club, you would've never done that with us" and mommy didn't say nothing like Yvette hadn't said a word.

At that same time all the stripping was going on, I finally got up with this dude named Claude who lived up stairs from me and had been stalking me since I was like eight or nine years old-real talk. He used to tell me all the time he wanted to show me some things and that he would have his way with me when I was older and I was feeling him, I had a crush on him-I was crazy young but he knew better! He was a fucking pervert now that I think about it; I mean what the fuck was he looking at back then? I didn't even reach puberty and you wanted to fuck me? That's some real pedophile shit.

Anyway I couldn't wait to get it popping with Claude, he was bald and light skin-almost to the point you would've considered him to be an albino. I know he had to have gotten teased all the time in the hood for being so light cause he had shell like finger nails and some odd knife shaped teeth, they had to get at him, you know how they do. Claude was thirty-nine at the time I began fucking with him, it was all good though, I didn't care he had a girl-he only got up with her on the weekend so the rest of the week was mine. He had a nice lil' Pathfinder in "99" which was cool plus the kid was packing a big dick and was convenient to fuck because he lived up stairs. The only thing that used to get me was he was always on some stalking shit; I mean since I was little this nigga wouldn't let anyone come next to me. Soon as I got back from my father's crib upstate he was on me, it was like he could smell me on my way, I wouldn't be surprised if he was just waiting to catch me coming through the door!

One day I came home from school and he was like, "Yo you wanna come up stairs and smoke a blunt with me?" It was all game; I wasn't as naive as he thought I knew we were going upstairs to get our fuck on. What his old perverted ass didn't know was this pretty young thing was going to put it on him and have him wide open! I sat on a bed that looked like he had since his teenage years and I started smoking the L and he stared eating my pussy, ahh now that's what I call relaxing. After he got enough of licking my clit he stood up and tried to put his dick in my mouth, I immediately pulled my head back like no-no, woa, that's not going down! I don't have anything against sucking dick but I wasn't into all that at that time. He didn't mind at that point because I'm sure he had plans on our relationship progressing to it and it did, we had a disastrous relationship but the sex was great.

We had set days when we would get up and fuck because Claude and his girl were together on the weekends so me and him did ours during the week. Not to mention his grown ass still lived with his moms and dad at damn near forty. I should have known something was wrong with that nigga, he basically possessed the mentality of a boy with the body of a man, what a shame, but he's not the only one, it effects a lot of men.

Some where in his warped mind he rationalized it was alright for him to hit women because he had always seen his mother verbally abusing his father. So Claude decided he carry on his family's tradition of abuse to the point he forced his wife to leave him. Unfortunately I didn't know any of this information regarding his past before hand even though everyone else did, I was a diamond in the rough and so many people hated it and left me out to dry. Fucking with Claude could've cost me my life on several occasions.

One day Claude was mad because we were arguing and I told him he should try being a man and then he slapped me in my ear so hard I almost went deaf! I had to go to his private doctor because of course I didn't have insurance at the time so I could get the blood clot removed from my ear after he slapped me. I would always find myself in the hands of one abuser to the next and I never knew why. It was like I could never get a break in that department, every relationship I had always started out so good but quickly turned sour. I always prayed and kept my faith in God no matter what I did or what was wrong because that was all I knew. Sometimes praying was the only thing that would ease the pain I felt, I prayed so hard at times I cried ... and I still do to this day. It surprises me at times I'm still a live, God knows I'm a survivor.

The blood clot isn't even half of the half; Claude hit me over the head with a fucking forty once of Old E! Luckily I had just gotten some pretty thick braids in my hair so it didn't penetrate but other then that who knows what my scalp would've looked like. I still managed to have little pieces of glass all in and throughout my shit! Then that bastard kicked me in my ass when I was hunched over in shock and believe it or not I didn't cry, I was just upset and hurt that I couldn't fight this nigga back because he was too strong! Back then I only weighed a about a buck thirty so you already know it was only but so much I could do, he was a grown ass diesel mother fucker! But trust and believe one night after I had a little too much to drink after I came home from the club I went Tina Turner status on his ass! That bitch tried to hit me and I went straight to his room where he kept his-gun and grabbed the burner and started pistol-whipping his ass! It felt good but at the same time he made me wish I hadn't done it because he snatched that gun out of my hand and chocked the shit out of me! The only thing I could think of was to say I loved him so he might have a little sympathy for me and let me go but he didn't even act like he was going for that. He said, "You don't love me bitch, you just saying that cause I have my hands around your fucking neck!" He was right; I hated him and would've probably killed him if I could and the only thing I could think of was, "God please save me." Once again God spared me but the suffering continued, after he finished chocking the shit out of me and I caught my breath. That evil nigga wouldn't even apologize or act like he cared, he wanted to fuck me, he actually told me, "Go lay on the bed so I can fuck you like the whore you are!" I couldn't believe this was happening to me, it's a wonder a bitch like me is still standing.

You know as odd as it seems the strip club became my getaway to forget about all the pain and problems I was dealing with in my life. In the strip club I felt powerful and wanted, not to mention it allowed me the chance to drink and make money, I loved it. Dancing provided me the perfect outlet to take all the negative energy I've absorbed and renew myself from within. I'll never forget one night I came home feeling it, I told my mother, "Ma I'm going to be famous one day cause I seen the competition and aint nobody touching me!" It was all a matter of time before I would be hanging out with celebrities on a regular basis and sleeping with them and turning them to celebrity stalkers and groupies ...

3

From Ashy to Classy

After my short-lived stay at Wiggles I moved on to Coco's Nest where a lot of prostitution went down then on to My Cousins in Brooklyn-don't ask me how they got the name but it was a cool spot. My Cousins was a slightly better upgrade then Wiggles and Coco's Nest for me, and more importantly it was where I really tighten my game on all levels! I started keeping my body fit and learned how to lure any nigga into spending all they had for what they all wanted ... and that was China Starr. The more time I spent at the club the more involved I became to the point when I did end up going to school I would dress like I would be going to work and I didn't give a fuck. I could careless about what any teacher had to say, they were talking about getting money after school was finished but I was getting it while I was still in the bitch so I was thinking, "what the fuck can you tell me?"

Once I was caking it I almost completely lost interest in school, like I said I already achieved the purpose of going to school so the only time I went was to floss because that was my naive mentality at the time. If I copped a new pair of kicks or a fly ass outfit I'd bless the halfway with my presence-other then that you'd hardy see me, Donna was gone and I began doing China fulltime ya feel me? My friends noticed the change in me and how couldn't you, I went from dusty tees to hurting they feelings something terrible, I was crushing them hard. Even though I was the center of attention when I showed my face, I still received a great deal of hate as expected. You'd think I'd have an easier time keeping my clothes on then taking them off! I swear it was just easier to stay home and sleep till noon and do it again then being in that hellhole. It wasn't like they were teaching us anything that would help us amount to anything so I left summer school and didn't think twice about it.

I had too much on my mind to worry about then to be dealing with shit that didn't make a big difference in my immediate future. Claude and I were still going at it damn near everyday and to make matters worse my moms knew and wouldn't do anything, she just basically stood by and watched as her seventeen year old daughter was being abused by a thirty-nine year old man, I mean "bastard." I couldn't believe that shit, I'm her daughter regardless of what else I may've did, I'm still her daughter and that's fucked up however you look at it. I was tired of Claude taking his insecurities out on me and always having to bare the results of his unhappiness from his personal life and bullshit ass operator job. I knew I needed to get away from Claude the psycho but I didn't know how I was gonna do it, and to top it off my job at My Cousins turned sour from sweet.

I got into a fight with some nobody ass bitch, I can't even remember her name she was so insignificant but she did have three girlfriends to hold her down when we fought. And I was never the type to run with a crew or be cliqued up so I was left to thug it out on my own and because I was by myself I was considered the weakest link. On top of that somebody snitched on me about my age and it was a wrap! It threw me off a minute when management told me there can't be any heat in the club and I had to go, but the Lord works in mysterious ways because on my way out I met some other girl who was being put out, for what I don't know-don't get me to lying.

Anyway as we were walking out to go our separate ways the girl said, "Ayo, if you're eighteen you can go with me to work at Sweet Cherry's, they'll let you work but you can't drink."

I was like aight even though I still wasn't eighteen I was a hustla and that's all I need to be, I got a fake i.d and I was back on the next day, I guess all the praying I did paid off. Sweet Cherry's ended up being a better situation for me and I couldn't complain, it was cleaner, the men couldn't touch us and prostitution wasn't allowed-even better I took half of My Cousins clientele because it wasn't too far from My Cousins and I never fucked a single one of them! The way I was getting money was like taking candy from a baby, I locked down Cherry's for about two and half years, it was nothing-Cherry's was mine.

As usual I stood out wherever I went so one day while I was downtown shopping in Fulton Street Mall and was about to catch a cab I hear somebody yell, "Ayo China, yo China!" My first thought was oh it must be one of my fans, he wasn't yelling my government so he had to know me from the club. I was right because when he caught up to me I asked him flat out, "Do I know you?"

I don't know why he thought I should've remembered him considering I met countless people a night who wanted me in some way or another so what did he think made him any different then the rest? Alright, he was standing there draped in diamonds iced the fuck out back in "99" way before a lot of niggas started to letting their chain hang low but I didn't know who he was but he seemed interesting.

"I met you at Cherry's, I gave you my number remember? My name is Shawn."

I just played it off, I had no fucking idea who he was, he just looked like he was fucking wit my man's and nem, you know Franklin and Hamilton-two of my favorite dead presidents, "Yea I remember you, hey Shawn what's up?"

Shawn invited me to go shopping with him and how can I resist that, he was paying! So I went along with the kid and he brought us both some Ice Burg shit and splurged like that's what's up. When Shawn pulled out a brolick knot of money I was like wow, should I rob this nigga? It caught me off guard, I wasn't expecting him to pull out something that yelled "what it do-what it do." I thought in this situation it was better to fall back and see where this unexpected meeting would take me, so once he dropped me off in some van he had cause his Lex got shot up I decided I'd link up with him some time soon after I returned from Florida.

I was on my to Florida to get money and get away from the New York State mind-well grind, you can never change your mind frame as a New Yorker. We hustle everywhere we go it's in our blood. Not having to deal with Claude's abuse and having the freedom and piece of mind to let my hair down I was able to get cake and actually enjoy it. When I got back to the hood it was the same shit as usual, I don't care how long you've been gone or where you live the hood never changes-the hood will always be the hood.

I decided to call Shawn up and see what he had lined up for the day and he happened to be free so we decided to get up. But what was funny about the whole situation was you know how everyone says everything happens for a reason? It's true I couldn't have planned it better I knew I had to brake free from Claude more and more each day that passed, especially after I started hearing rumors of him being a former hit man. And the way our relationship was going I could've easily been a victim sooner or later. Claude had a daughter damn near my age and I heard through word of mouth and local gossip around the way the only way his ex-wife was able to get rid of him was by getting some dude bigger then him, because he wasn't about to hit a man whether his life depended on it. Word on the street was Claude was pussy and couldn't fight to save his life so he kept a burner on him at all times incase anything ever popped off.

Check it—Claude was driving through the block most likely in search for me as expected and spots me getting into Shawn's Lexus and just drove right by! No static or nothing, he just kept it moving, knowing how Shawn got down, Claude was never a factor at all in my life again from that point on. Just like that God took me out of one situation and placed me into the next, I guess he felt I suffered long enough and it was time to learn another lesson.

One day I was visiting my girlfriend Milky I meet from work at Cherry's and her roommate's friend Dave came by and told us he needed a stripper to dance for his boy who was a friend of Ed Lover for his birthday. I already told Dave and Milky I was done with Claude and was in serious heat and horny as hell and was down for whatever, so I got the job. It was understood from the beginning this was going to be a one and done deal between Ed and I, so not too long later Dave called me one afternoon and was like, "China we need to go up to Hot 97 and see Ed Lover" and it was on!

Dave gave me $200 and I did the rest, when I entered the station I went to the bathroom to change into a one-piece neon green teddy outfit and a pair of black pattern leather thigh high boots, and came out crushing 'nem! After I was dressed some guys took me to a room Ed Lover was chilling in and opened the door so we could start the show. I walked up to Ed laying on a bed dressed in a multi-colored Coogi sweater and matching hat and huddled over him and said, "Happy birthday Ed Lover!" As soon as we caught eye contact I immediately began riding him with my clothes on and trust me, he loved every minute of it! Until some nosey ass came in the room with a camcorder and started recording me on top of him. Ed got up immediately and snatched the camera from the dude and locked the door shut so we could have some privacy.

It wasn't long after that I was grinding my pussy up against Ed's face and he was pulling my g-string to the side and munching on my pussy like he was the first disciple at the last supper! I loved how he stuck his tongue out and licked in between my split and rotated it round and round then up and down my super sensitive clit. Oh my god he got my clit so damn hard! I lie to you not, I could not wait to get fucked my pussy was so saturated. But instead of giving it to me like I wanted, Ed picked me up and placed me on top of an office table and continued to devour my pussy for what seemed like hours, it was like he just couldn't stop eating it and I wasn't mad at him, he was killing that shit!

The longer he ate my pussy the wetter it got, after a while I started to make my clit jump so he could feel it moving in his mouth like it had a mind of its own. Then on another level with every stroke of his tongue I kept my clit in rhythm with his motion until my whole body got hot and legs started uncontrollably trembling. At that point I knew I was almost where I needed to be so I cocked my pussy in the air for him to get every drop of sweet juice that fell from my clit to his mouth as I came all down his throat and in his mouth! That shit felt so damn good I couldn't take it anymore, even though I loved it-I had to tell him to stop! Ed Lover's head game is official, matter fact you still don't know how hard I came that night!

Ed had to bounce so we didn't fuck but it was far from over, Dave called me later that same night and told me Ed Lover was performing at Caroline's Comedy Club in Manhattan and wanted me to meet him there, it was no problem so I did. When I got to the club I realized just how big Ed's balls are when he not only invited me to the same spot his wife would be, but went public announcing him and his wife had a baby on the way. He even had the nerve to introduce her to the crowd! The whole time I'm thinking to myself, a few hours ago this nigga just finished eating my pussy like he was a famished African and now me and his wife are in the same room as if nothing ever happened. I didn't really care whether or not she was there or not, actually the shit was funny to me, but at the same time I thought it was mad sneaky and reckless. I knew for a fact that by the end of the night I was gonna have him, so why stress it? She was the one married to him I was just there for the night.

So as time went on and Caroline's came to a close Dave drove me to a club where Ed Lover and I where going to really meet up and settle our unfinished business. After Ed finally dropped wifey off he eventually showed up at the club and it wasn't long after that we ended up back at Hot 97 going at it again. This time around we shared a little more intimacy, Ed took his time and laid me on a bed in another office and gave me a full body massage. First he started with my ass and thighs until he worked his way up to my neck and down all over again and I loved every ounce of it! Once again he ate my pussy for about an hour, then he told me he didn't want to use a condom to fuck me because he wanted to feel all my "sweet wet pussy." Normally I would've thought differently but I was young and in heat, we did it raw, hey you live and you learn. After we fucked doggy style on an office table in the room we went back around to the car garage for him to get in his white Benz and he put me in a cab and we went our separate ways.

It was still early in the night so I'm sure he went back to his wife like nothing happened and made it look as if he couldn't have done much in such a short time frame and really he didn't. I mean the sex was aight but the head was off the chain! We didn't continue anything from there because I didn't feel a strong sexual attraction between me and Ed so I left it as a one shot deal, but still I want to wish you a happy birthday Ed Lover and many more to come! LOL.

During the time I had my run in with Ed Lover and meeting with Shawn I was constantly traveling in and out of New York and Florida getting money and living it up. I was still getting it at Sweet Cherry's and another spot I danced at in Fort Lauderdale called Peek-A-Boo. You already know nobody was fucking with me in absolutely no form or fashion out there neither! Not even Peebles, oh my bad-Gloria Velez, one of Aaron Hall's baby moms and known video vixen and biting ass bitch. She stole mad shit from me, from dance moves to shaking her ass cheeks while standing in place. If it weren't for me them bitches would still be just taking their clothes off rolling around collecting dollars. Since I aint been around times have changed, did you notice in Game's "Wouldn't Get Far" video all she did was sit in the car? I wasn't around to show her how to dance so she ran out of moves and sat down, point and case, it is what it is.

I'm not saying I'm the pioneer of the strip game but when I did come through the doors of Peek-A-Boo's, I showed them how to blend dancing and stripping together like Twizzlers and they all followed. That's my word I got bitches in Brooklyn to this day trying to learn my shit, I always been a trendsetter even down to my outfits. I had a girl named Coco lacing me with nothing but the hottest shit, at the time the average outfit would run you about twenty-five to thirty dollars and it would be made out of a basic material nothing exclusive or much to brag about, you know all around generic. But Coco took it to another level, true story, my girl's clothes where custom made and fitted to the shape of your body like it was poured on and she could give it to you however you envisioned. Every outfit she did was made out of nothing but the best and would run you anywhere from eighty to ninety dollars easy but it was well worth the money. If you weren't getting it or wasn't serious about the game in a major way you was fucking with off the rack shit from local lingerie stores. Since I'm a go-getter I had no problem spending extra cheese, because trust me it all came back.

Anyway, I don't know for what reason but one day in the dressing room Gloria began spilling her guts out to me and decided to tell me that Aaron Hall's her baby's father and she was taking care of their child by herself without him and blah, blah, blah like I cared or gave a fuck. Not saying that trying to be rude but we never clicked like that so what was the point in telling me, we weren't friends. She even went as far as digging into her duffle bag to show me a picture of her son that she kept with her, I was just like "cute but I don't do those" meaning kids. I was young, fly and getting money while they were hating, why would I give a fuck? I just figured she knew I was a bad bitch from Up Top and since Aaron was famous for hanging out at strip clubs in the area, I'd probably meet him one day so she'd shit on his name. Either that or she really wanted me to have some sort of sympathy for her sorry ass story, it was her problem and either way I could careless. I grabbed my girl Vanessa and we was back to Brooklyn.

When I got back I began spending more time with Shawn and getting to know him and increasingly becoming spoiled and loving it because he gave me pretty much whatever I wanted! The great thing about Shawn was with him money wasn't a thing if he had it-it was nothing to spend it. Granted I wasn't attracted to Shawn but he was kind hearted and definitely generous, so it didn't really matter. He grew on me. I vowed to myself after fucking with Claude I would never date another broke mother fucker again, if all niggas gonna cheat and make demands and shit, why not get something out of it? I could thank Claude for that, he wasn't the first one to beat me but he did change me. Fuck that, I'll be damned if it ever goes down like that again.

I kid you not, I'd say at the most a week after Gloria cried me a river I was back to business in Cherry's when Vanessa comes up to me and tells me Aaron Hall was in the building! I was like get the fuck out here and you know me, I'm about my ends so I dipped off back into the dressing room to grab something a little more seductive and enticing. Of course it worked, before I finished my set he walked up to me with a hand full of twenty-dollar bills and instructions to see him when I was done and I did and from there our story began …

4

Eating My Cake

I began dating Aaron Hall and Shawn at the same time enjoying the best of both worlds: Aaron had good dick and Shawn had money, I couldn't loose. I had everything any women could ask for, I was having great sex, which is highly important to me I had lots of money, jewelry and plenty of clothes to match! I was still enjoying stripping, I stayed fit and had fun every night I worked. I used drugs and drank alcohol all the time because it went hand and hand with stripping, and enjoyed every bit of my life without bills because I was still staying with my moms. It seemed like Shawn and Aaron was racing to see who could get me pregnant first but I had other plans, I was keeping my options open. Neither one of them were my man and I could do what I wanted to do so I was fine right where I was at and had no interest in wearing handcuffs. The relationship was new with the both of them, and I figured I had to kiss a couple of frogs to meet my prince.

Me and Aaron had crazy sex; we used to go at it for hours on a regular basis! When I say hours—I mean hours, I'm not just saying hours cause it sounds good, we use to fuck hard-body. I fucked Shawn here and there but it was nothing near how me and Aaron got down, we were more like hangout buddies. If I could have figured out how to put Aaron's dick on Shawn I would've been in heaven cause I'm not going to lie to you ... size means everything to me, the bigger the better except in Cincere's case, his shit was too big. Shawn's dick is probably about nine inches and Aaron's is about twelve, yes three inches does make a difference, some of ya'll know. I'm telling you although I had Aaron all the time I could never get used to it so it was a challenge for me every time we did it and we were like rabbits when it came down to it! Truthfully he was way too much for me, I was only nineteen at the time and his dick was so big he couldn't put the whole thing all the way in me because it hurt me so damn bad. Aaron said he didn't date anything over twenty-five, that's why he wasn't even trying to get back with Gloria cause she was already twenty-five back in 2000. Leave it to her she's still under thirty, lol. I figured since I'm not going to stay young forever I might as well start a family with someone more stable, because consistency is a very important part to me in relationships so I leaned more so to Shawn in that department.

Aaron Hall's sex drive was crazy as hell! Every Monday we would meet at the Parker Meridien Hotel back when he was going to anger management class every Monday in downtown Brooklyn somewhere. Soon as I'd step through the door it was on, he'd rip my clothes completely off till I was ass naked and sit me in a chair and just eat me out. Sometimes he'd eat for five or six hours, it was one of his favorite things to do to me with no question. Let me tell you something, Ed Lover was official but lets get one thing clear, Aaron Hall gives the best head in the world hands down, celebrity or no celebrity he gives the best brain I ever had. I guarantee you a porn star would tell you there's nothing like it! He knew I loved it so much he would tease me by saying little things like if I wasn't a good girl he wouldn't give me any head, so let's just say I was on my best behavior at all times, inside voice and all. I was in love with the way he fucked me and without saying I was open!

Me and Aaron had a great relationship, he knew about Shawn and I and he told me all about the baby he just had with some girl. As a matter of fact I remember him fucking me in the Meridien from the back when he was on the phone with her once, it was so damn funny, I wanted to laugh the whole time but I didn't want him to get knocked but you should've saw my face. Aaron used to swear he never dealt with a girl who had a man but me and Shawn was close enough so what was he saying? Nothing, but it didn't matter because I loved Aaron and I have nothing bad to say about him. Gloria knew about us because that bitch Vanessa ran back to Florida and told her, I knew I shouldn't have fucked with her. I just wanted to see what it was like to be with a woman on that level so we dated briefly but it wasn't for me, I didn't see the point of getting ate out then fucked with a strap on. I'm sorry plastic's not going to work I need the real thing.

During the time I was seeing Aaron and going back and forth to Fort Lauderdale, according to Aaron him and Gloria were in the middle of a custody battle for their son. It pissed him off that Gloria was stripping under the name Pebbles because their son's name is Bam Bam-you know like the kid from The Flintstones, so he was tight. Knowing that I knew her and didn't give two fucks about her he paid me to take a picture of her in the club and I did, I caught her in the dressing room naked with a bruise on her leg. She knew what I was doing to cause she yelled, "I know you didn't just take a picture of me!" I was like, "Don't nobody want to take a picture of you!" and kept it moving, I was really wishing she had the nerves to try and grab my camera so I could have at least one reason to whip her ass worse then Remy Ma did! I couldn't stand that bitch-I still can't stand that bitch.

Let me tell you, I've been waiting to get at Pebbles since that day I was talking to Ice-T at the exit of the club about who I was with regarding stripping in Florida, because he was interested in taking me with him on some business shit but because I was messing with an agency I couldn't go. Other then that who knows? Well Gloria must've gotten mad Ice-T was playing me close after all the talking she was doing to him throughout the night and by the end he was hollering at me. Being the hatter she is her stupid ass tried pushing me as she went by so I grabbed a hand full of her long blonde weave and pulled a track out that bitch and all she did was just keep going like nothing happened! I'm telling you she never wanted it, at least she was smart enough not to get her ass beat, that's all I can say. She's a hater, a wanna be mini me and could never beat my ass-so no I never had a problem fucking the brains out her baby's daddy.

Our relationship lasted from about late 1999 until early 2000 and it wasn't solely based on sex, we shared a lot emotionally. There were times when he would cry on my shoulders and tell me all about his problems and express how he felt about his domestic problems and other issues in his life. At that time I wasn't used to seeing men cry so at first I wanted to laugh but I got used to it and was there for him. I loved Aaron all though I knew he had many children and was nowhere near being the type of man capable of being a great father to my child if I were to have one, which was important to me though we never discuss it. I didn't want a bastard child nor did I want to end up another one of his sorry ass baby mammas, I just couldn't see it, I wanted more. I grew up without my dad barely being there, so I wanted better for my child. I saw there was potential with Shawn because he was a good father, he took care of his children and made sure his son Dayshawn and daughter Shawna were well taken care of. I felt even if me and Shawn didn't live together my child would be secure and that's all that mattered to me, there wasn't away I was going to allow my child to be born into poverty like I was.

So when I did end up pregnant with Aaron's child I didn't tell him, I was not trying to end up like Gloria or the rest of them. The day before I was going to have the abortion I went to visit him at his room in the Marriott in downtown Brooklyn and he could tell something was wrong but not quite cause I never told. I think he had a feeling I may've been pregnant because when I told him I wanted to see him that day but couldn't stay because I had an appointment in the morning, he got on his knees crying and begged me to stay before I left. I felt so bad but I couldn't bare it, I wasn't trying to be a single mother. Looking back on it today, I regret what I did, I look at things differently and I would've adapted to the situation, it might not have been that bad. I loved him and I'm sure our baby would've even been the joy of my life whether he was there or not.

We carelessly lost touch on Valentines Day because my mother's number changed and it slipped my mind to give it to him and ironically he had just gotten a new cell number, which I forgot to grab on my way out the hotel. Things happen for a reason but I can't help but wonder what things could've been like between us had we taken the time to exchange numbers. He dropped me off to my house in a limo one time so I'm sure he didn't remember where I lived. Down the road when I was working at Passions word got back to me that Aaron was looking for me, but a few people different had told me he was now a pimp and it wouldn't be a good look for me to get back with him, so I didn't pursue it. I left it at what we had, which was something good and that's how I like to remember him.

Shawn lived with another woman at first although he tried denying it for the first three months by saying she was his sister and her and his baby moms was close and that he knew if she got smart with me or came off fly I would bust her ass. It all seemed a little too shaky for me but he was right, I would've busted her ass if necessary so I played my position and kept him in my back pocket. I had no problem doing me; fuck it, why not it worked for me.

It wasn't until down the road me and Shawn started moving forward and trying to make things work and take our relationship to another level beyond hanging out and having sex occasionally. I wasn't seeing Aaron anymore so my time was devoted to Shawn and my job, where desperate customers wanted to spend big money for an eye candy fantasy. I learned after awhile finically Shawn is great but emotionally trust me he sucks! At first when we decided to settle down and try to start a family everything was gravy, not much to complain about. I found out he's a program nigga meaning any and everything has to be planned out if it's not he can't think straight let alone function. It's extremely hard for him to adapt to new situations, actually its damn near impossible. By the time I realized all this I was in way too deep, he has to suffer from an anti-social disorder. I'm no physiatrist but he does fit every characteristic for someone who has the disease. People like Shawn that are labeled with anti-social disorder have no remorse for anything they do! I took psychology in college and passed with an A-plus because I was so curious on how come people behave the way they do. Shawn will beat you in the head with something; any hard object he can pick up and the next day blame it on you as if it was your fault for his outburst! There is no reason for someone to put their hands on you, if they don't like what they see, they should just simply move on. Any reason a man gives you for domestic violence is just an excuse to continue to take their anger out on you. He wouldn't even apologize for his actions, not that it mattered, he would just think nothing of it as if the shit he does only affects him and no one else. All of them have problems with drugs and alcohol like he does and never talks to anybody, Shawn and I rarely spoke. Even when we hung all we did was drink and floss and later fuck but that was it, I can hardly remember him having a deep conversation with anyone.

I couldn't believe after I visited him every Friday and Saturday and put money in his convisery when he was locked up and he got out his ungrateful ass had the nerves to cheat on me with prostitutes while I was pregnant! I was walking around with holes in my shoes unable to work and he was out allegedly spending $400.25 cent on pussy and coming home and fucking me! I aint one to talk cause I did it too but I wasn't putting my child in danger and I was getting paid to fuck niggas like him, but what the fuck was the 25 cent for, a surcharge! At that point he wasn't even taking care of things at home, he was fucking up big time, he was doing shit right across the board.

After all that I gave up for Shawn he couldn't give up tricking for me? At the least I should've had a decent pair of shoes on my feat in the freezing snow! At that point in my life I was so depressed I contemplated killing myself because I couldn't take the frustration and pain any longer. Normally I would get drunk or high but because I was pregnant all I could do was cry and even that wasn't helping the baby, my stomach was constantly in knots. If I was sad the baby was sad and it was nothing I could do about it. So at my lowest point during my pregnancy I grabbed a chair from the table and reached for the gloc on top of my entertainment center and sat on the floor and took the gun off safety and was about to pull the trigger when my mother called me. She said Shawn came by and told her I was tripping and she needed to check on me so she called, thank God cause I was the one tripping? If he had not been out fucking hoes and acting so irresponsibly I wouldn't have been attempting suicide! My mother told me everything would be fine after I had the baby and I could go back to doing for myself again, and I thought to myself, you know what she's right so I never did it.

I was determined not to let him get the best of me, I may have blown up to 250 pounds but I was sure as hell going to make him wish he never played me. I was going to make it a point to be stronger and better then I was at any point before I became pregnant and I meant it. On May 18, 2001 I gave birth to my beautiful baby girl, Tatiana who is now the love of my life! Through all the bullshit I went through, I would not turn back the hands of time if I could all because of her, she is a blessing and I can't imagine my life without her. With all the drama I've been through and continue to go through she is the only thing that's gave my life meaning.

Having Tatiana helped me to feel what real love is, Tatiana loves me unconditionally because I'm me, not because I'm pretty or my pussy is good. She loves Donna not China Starr the money getter. There is no one capable of separating the closeness we share; I've been through poverty, rape, domestic violence and abandonment and some how I've managed to come out whole through the grace of God! After all that I've been through, my proudest moment was when I gave birth to my child … I'd give her the world.

5

Back On My Grind

After Tatiana arrived a lot of things changed, I went back to dancing immediately to bring my weight back down and plenty of ecstasy to boost, in two months I was down to 150 easy and working at Passion's strip club. I didn't go back to Sweet Cherry's because about three months deep into my pregnancy shit got crazy, obviously I had a problem at any club I danced at because I was the center of attention and most bitches couldn't stand it but the shit just hit the fan.

With no regrets I put my time in at Sweet Cherry's so it was weird letting it go but let me explain what caused me to end my run at my home away from home. One night right when I was just about ready to get off stage some hating nobody ass bitch who had a sister that worked there as well wanted to step out her place. She was two different people, when her sister was there with her she was certified gangsta but in reality on any other occasion she was more ass then the club, anyway she felt like she could tell me to get off the stage! Who the fuck did she think she was talking to, not me, time is money so I told her, "I have ten more minutes wait your turn." I knew I was pregnant and couldn't work much longer so I figured I go out with a bang after her punk ass tried to threaten me talking about, "When my sister comes back we gonna jump you!" Oh really, imagine that, I figured I cut to the chase and beat her ass before her sister got there and she could tell her about it, I'll be damned if I let her get the drop on me. I don't know if that bitch was drunk or high and really didn't care but I know one thing, when her ass kept coming towards that stage I grabbed her by her throat and pushed her back and said, "You better get off this fucking stage." But she kept coming, it was like she was just begging to get her ass whipped so I happily gave her what she was asking for ... the next time I saw her coming I hung onto the pole real tight to get a good grip and kicked the shit out of her stomach while she went flying over the banister and onto the floor. You should've saw her, she tried to get up but them big ass boots she had on that went all the way up to hers knees wouldn't let her so I jumped off the stage and got busy. I grabbed a few Heineken bottles from somewhere and busted her in the head with every last one of them while everybody watched you think anybody was trying to help that bitch! Strippers don't look cute all cut up! The bouncers eventually carried the bitch to the owner's office cause I was about to leave her laid the fuck out! Do you know after she got some sort of consciousness she was banging all over Mike's door talking bout "don't hold me back" after all that space and opportunity she had before I got in that ass. Please, that bitch aint want it, she was scared shitless. Mike was a sweet dude and asked me what happened without accusing me and all so I told him the truth! Now normally I would have made up some excuse like she hit me first or give some long ass, but since I knew in my mind I had already decided I was out so I quit that night. I told the owner Mike, "That bitch had it coming to her for a long time, so I gave it to her ass!" And that's why I went to Passions after my baby was born.

Shawn wasn't feeling I was getting money and looking good after the baby and we began going through it even more, I gave the ring back and said fuck him, I was tired of our make believe relationship. Some how I found myself in the middle of Spanish Harlem and at one point holding down my daughter, four cousins and helped my aunt catch up on her back rent. Once again it was only a matter time I would get into some sort of trouble because I'm a fly bitch in the middle of Spanish Harlem and I did. At that time all the girls around my way were dressing like tomboys so I thought to myself I'ma change my style up for a while to stick out and killed it! I said I'd be damned if any fucking female's going to have me walking around looking like a fucking boy just to make them feel better about themselves. Self-esteem is a "self" problem not China problem so I kept my fucking look up and figured I'd deal with any problem as it came as usual.

I came down the block one day "stuntin like my daddy" and literally caused a riot ... fire trucks, police cars and ambulances and the whole nine-they was all there! I was coming from the liquor store minding my own business so I could get my drink on and relax with my big bottle Alize I just bought when I bumped into a local stalker by the name of G-Dep. Mr. Special Delivery saw me walking by and approached me on some, "yo let's go smoke a blunt." So I was like alright we could do that, so me, him and a friend of his got in a black jeep G-Deep had and smoked what I assumed was some good ass weed, but come to find out really it wasn't!

Rumor has it he's a notorious dust head but back then I didn't know so I burned with him, if I would've known better I wouldn't have smoked anything I didn't see him roll. I started feeling real funny then extremely horny and I knew it wasn't because of him. G-Dep asked me I don't know how many times before to suck his dick and I always said no, matter of fact "hell no" not even just that day. So I had no idea why I just felt like fucking, I remember I just kept feeling helpless, horny and weird. I assume he was desperate to get his dick sucked because desperate times call for desperate measures and lacing a blunt for some head is one of them.

Well anyway the three of us went to the car wash and then back to the projects, on the ride back some how or another G-Dep and I ended up in the back seat of the jeep while his friend drove. Being in an uncontrollable horny state I began sucking his dick, I was surprised it was actually big and fat and right when I was getting into it sucking the head, I heard a bang on the back passenger side door. When I looked up there were two girls standing outside the truck yelling, "get out the car, get out the car!" So I got out the fucking car with my bottle of Alize and as soon as my foot touched the floor I hit one of them bitches with the bottle, while the other girl tried to pull my hair. It was nothing but the grace of God I had on a jaw string ponytail so the bitch couldn't get a good grip of my hair! I bounced after that cause them bitches was not gonna ware my ass out! Those bitches were so damn fat it was no way possible they could keep up with me, bitch I was out!

I had to jump over a few gates to get to what was considered the PR side of the block, which I didn't know at the time, which really didn't make a difference cause I didn't give a damn cause if I had to I'd do it again!

By time I got to the other side and ran across the street, to my cousin's building they were all laid up at the pool so I had to fend for self. They had to have seen me or knew where I was at because when I came down stairs there were about ten girls trying to fight me, damn, you would've thought I got caught sucking the president's dick! You know me I was thinking to myself I have to get to some bottles so I ran to the pizza shop on 125th and Lexington Ave. barefooted. I would turn around as I was running and start waving at them like catch up bitches, lol, because little did they know what the fuck I had in store for their asses.

As soon as I entered the fucking pizza shop I jumped over the counter and found a cordless phone and speed dialed 911 and told the operator I was being chased by a bunch of bitches like I was J-Lo on the block being stalked by paparazzi and they needed to get their asses down their a-s-a-p! Shit I aint got no bodyguards, lol. After I got off the phone some crazy ass employee of the pizza shop suggested I go into the basement and wait for the cops. I was like, "You must be fucking crazy, I'm not about to die in a dirty ass basement waiting for the cops", so I told him maybe he'd better go down there cause I was about to get it poppin!

It wasn't even a full five minutes until the crowd arrived at the pizza shop's door when I saw a garbage can filled with ice cold Snapple's to the rim, bingo! I was back at it like a crack addict fresh from rehab with his stem in hand when I spotted them colorful bottles, I started attacking each that came threw! Talk about make it rain, I brought hurricane Katrina to their ass and definitely cleared that mother fucker out! I aint care who got hit and for everybody out there who wanted to stand around and watch I gave them a show! As I pitched Snapple's the girls tried to protect themselves with pizza pans until I eventually ran out. One of the girls managed to get over the counter but I found one Snapple bottle that didn't break and hit G-Dep's baby's mother in the stomach with it! As we began fighting I started to bite my nails in half so I could turn the acrylic into knives, then I started digging my fingers into her eyes. And then all of a sudden I felt some one pull me through a window to the right of the pizza shop and drooped me on the floor!

I don't know who snatched me out the window but I got up and ran out into the middle of the street trying to flag a cab down and I got one, I grabbed the door to a cab that never stopped! I was still holding the door even though it jerked me a little and at that point the cops finally came and brought an ambulance. At first a cop came out to me and asked me did I want to be put on a stretcher and I was like, "Hell fucking no I don't fucking need one!" I didn't need a damn stretcher or anybody assistance and I definitely wasn't going to give those bitches the impression I did neither. I walked over to the ambulance and got in by fucking self, it was a shame it took that many of them to try to contain my little ass and I was still standing!

I had to stay for a little while but I was okay-it was nothing major so I left the same day. I told my baby's daddy Shawn to come pick me up and when Shawn came and got me all he could manage to say was, "You got what you deserved!" I was in shock in total disbelief because here I am the mother of his child regardless of the situation I was almost killed by a mob of fat bitches and a cab driver who didn't want to stop and all he can say to me is I got what I deserved! I had to leave it in God's hands it was nothing else I could do.

Actually a similar situation happened to Hi when he got jumped by a bunch of bodyguards at this club called Pook-Knockers on Atlantic Ave. that was famous for knocking niggas wigs the fuck off! Hi got away by grabbing a truck passing by and ended up dragging him for two blocks strong, it was either that or end up getting bodied because the situation got completely out of hand! You never know what you'll do in a life or death situation until you're in it; I swear life is crazy-fuck a box of chocolate's, Forrest Gump wasn't from the hood!

The whole situation was ironic and fucked up because during one of the many times Shawn had a "feeling" I was trying to leave him he tried to set me up to get me jumped at this restaurant we used to go to all the time. First he got me super drunk, I mean certified fucked up and placed our order with the owner's wife which he knew envied me. Then he decides he wants to pick up our food all the way at the end of the night and as soon as she says she didn't put the order in he puts the battery in my back to spit in her face knowing damn well when I'm saucey I wouldn't hesitate to do it!

Without words being spoken the code of the street is when you do shit like that, you keep it moving-you don't just stand there and wait to what's going to happen next, shit you already know what's ganna happen-so I dipped! I kept telling Shawn's back stabbing ass to come on and let's go, but he was obviously waiting to see something bad happened to me and saucey or not I could smell bullshit before it pops off. Shawn's old ass wasn't born yesterday and he's from the hood so he knew the consequences of my actions so if he wanted to stand around and catch the back lash-let him. I gave him time to get his shit together because I believe in the code of "we came together, we live together" when shit goes down. So I played the sidewalk for about three minutes when a bouncer came outside and put a bug in my ear like, "Ayo China I really like you and if you want to continue looking good, I suggest you keep it moving cause all those girls inside are talking about coming out here and jumping you and cutting up your face and shit." Still trying to hold that mother fucker Shawn down I told my boy, "Well tell Shawn to come on!" When he told me Shawn said come back inside I was like I'm out, fuck that, I aint no fucking Foxy!

I didn't want to leave him but I wasn't trying to be toothless like he was about to be neither, I couldn't believe he was going out on me like that and I never did shit to him. Regardless of our differences when it came situations like that I always had his back but that's aight, God don't like ugly. Lucky for me around the time all this was poppin of some nigga was trying to holla at me in a car and I was able to take advantage of the situation and use his ass for my get away driver. Shiiiit call me whatever you like but you can't tell me I aint a mother fucking survivor, I made it out that bitch alive without a single fucking scratch.

The next day I got a call from Shawn telling me he was in the hospital and he got fucked up real bad and I felt sorry for him. Even though he wanted me to look so fucked up that nobody would want to look at my face, I'm not as cold hearted as him and I had some sympathy for him. I don't know why I cared how he was doing because he obviously didn't give a fuck about me, but I called my moms and told her what happened and what I was going through and she surprisingly brought me to my senses! I know of all people right, lol. After I told her how bad I felt, my moms was like, "I don't know why you feeling sorry for him because if it were Shawn he'd be very happy right now." That's when I realized she was right, when I got fucked up in Harlem he had no fucking remorse for me so why should I feel bad, at least when he called me I didn't tell him he deserved it which he did! He shouldn't have been trying to fucking set me up! Good for his fucking ass, oh yea by the way Shawn, "You fucking deserved it!"

Oh yea, so getting back to the situation that took place Uptown, no one comforted me until the next day when I told my homeboy C-Love what happened to me, no one else seemed to care. Everybody just went about their business like "fuck China", I was fucking frustrated as hell and left to suffer alone by myself once again and since old habits diehard and something's never change I wrote a couple verses to ease the pain, here's a couple bars I dropped from "116th and Lex" ...

"Ask bitches, they will never forget/how I spazzed out on one hundred and sixteen and fucking Lex/in the pizza shop throwing Snapple's like tech's/bitches using pizza pans for vest/they can't test, yo, Brooklyn's the best/fuck the south or the north/or the east, or the west/uh/it's the east/we eat niggas like beast/born New York Rican, projects, and concrete/you can feel the heat right under your feet/the devil's working over time in these here rough streets"

I aint even gonna give ya'll the whole shit right now but I did the whole song in about five minutes-true story. Unfortunately all that was just the beginning of even rougher times to come, I'm telling you watch the company you keep because they'll cause you to loose a lot and can cost you your life if you let them. I began drinking and doing more ecstasy and coke then I had in the past and really started loosing control. I found myself in one fucked up situation after the next and Shawn wasn't making anything better. Since my safe home was ruined by those hating ass Harlem bitches I had to move back to Brooklyn and around Shawn once again, and he was way too about it too.

Shawn would drop me off at C-Love's house with my one year old knowing he would be sniffing coke around me and I could eventually fall victim to circumstance among other things and without saying it went down. All he wanted to do was drop the baby and me off so he could run the streets and do his dirt regardless of whatever else was going on. No I shouldn't be getting high and there isn't an excuse but at the same time Shawn was fully aware of the situation and let it happened and if you want to be technical, he was the main cause of it. I think he wanted me to end up strung out and end up being nothing but a bum ass junkie un-capable of taking care of myself or Tatiana so he could take her from me and move her in with that bitch he was living with. She was too old to have any kids of her own so he figured since Tatiana was so young she'd forget about me and Janette could raise her as her child and my daughter would think she was her mom. As fucked up as it sounds I honestly believe that was what he was hoping for because one day Shawn actually fixed his face to say, "I know you're getting high with your friend over there" and when I said, "Well why do you keep dropping me and your daughter off over there then?" Shawn had nothing to say ... we both knew the answer and it was nothing left to discuss, sad as it sounds it's all true. Fuck it, we both was wrong, I'll admit I was young but you live and you learn. Shawn was just playing mind games with me but I'm a strong willed person so it was ganna take more then that to bring me down, but he kept on!

For no other reason then he just wanted to start some shit, Shawn came home pushing me for no reason and bighting my fur! Why the would you put a fucking fur coat in your mouth, a mother fucker aint never been that hungry. Crazy yes, hungry never, it was all part of his plan. He knew I was high and knew I wasn't gonna let Tatiana see all that so like he knew I would I called the fucking cops, I was wilding. Of all times for the cops to actually come quick they choose that night when I was twisted, it might not have been that bad because I could've probably played it off but Shawn knew the fucking cop so it was a wrap, I was fucked beyond fucked!

When the police got to my house, the house was a mess and I was completely out my element. I believe Shawn fucked her before so I had no wins and was completely loosing my mind. I couldn't believe that shit-why me? Shawn's little officer friend had the nerve to tell him in front of my face, "Well Shawn it looks like you have two kids on your hands." You don't know how upset that made me, but I had enough sense in me to remember she was a cop and cursing her out wasn't going to do me any good. I would've been at her ass immediately and got locked up for assault and some more shit. Don't think I didn't think about it a couple of times especially after they both sat their asses in my living room talking about me and laughing like I'm a dog. After about an hour of them disrespecting me I decided I say something cause I couldn't take it any more it was driving me crazy, I really needed to be high at that point, I mean damn an hour-take that shit somewhere else! I wasn't even high anymore, fuck; go about your damn business already. I told Shawn and the cop to let me know when they were finished having fun and would you know them bitches carried on! I know it's wrong and everybody gonna say China's wrong for saying this but I understand why a lot of cops get shot ... they're assholes.

She even asked Shawn why doesn't he just take my daughter to live with him and his girl? Still, like they are not discussing my life in my house where I rest my head-Shawn tells officer high-n-mighty his girl was willing to do it but it just wasn't the time yet! Right then and there I knew Shawn and Janette had to have talked about taking my baby from me before hand! When he said that his true colors finally came out, ehw! Talking about it right now just makes me mad, I swear I wish she wasn't a cop; I wanted to beat their asses so bad. I told that nosey ass cop he's not willing to take the responsibility of fully raising a child and he's only interested in keeping tabs on me that's why he even left her in my custody in the first place. I wasn't fucked up enough "yet", I would have had to been a beat up ugly looking junky before he would have taken his daughter. He was damn sure trying to make it happen as fast as he could by taking me to C-Love's house everyday faithfully.

If I gave Shawn Tatiana it would've gave me too much free time on my hands to do whatever I wanted and trust me that's the last thing Mr. Shawn wanted me to do. He'd try to trap me by all means necessary, that's why we had a child in the first place, he used her to keep me. Soon as I told my moms we were planning on having a baby she told me it was a trap but you can't tell a nineteen year old nothing, once again I had to learn the hard way.

Damion Hall Teddy Riley Aaron Hall

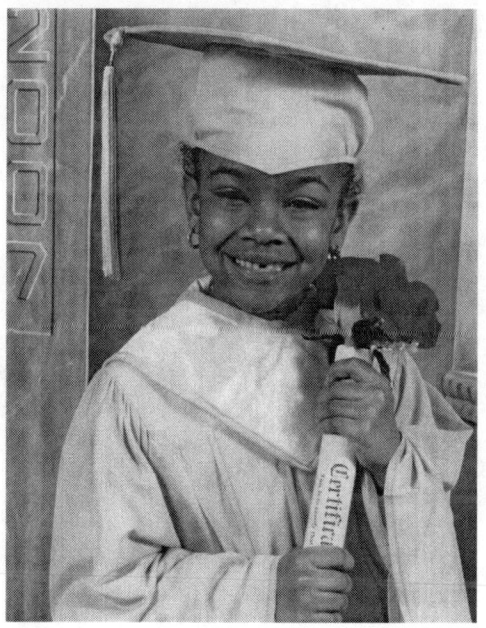

6

Waking Up To Reality

By time 2005 rolled around I had more then enough of living like a child, I wasn't able to have any company in "the house", I wasn't on the lease and couldn't do a damn thing without Shawn's go. He used his money to control me and he made sure to remind me every chance he got. Let Shawn tell it if I went out with any of my friends I was cheating on him and when I returned to my so-called "home" the locks would be changed. The nigga is a lunatic, sometimes I would be left with no choice but to seek shelter anywhere I could, which really wasn't a problem, what man wouldn't want to lay up with me for at least a night? But having a spot to rest a few days if necessary wasn't the issue, I just hated being placed in situations like that because niggas take advantage of shit like that all the time. When someone feels you need them instead of showing you compassion and sympathy they treat you like shit and give you their ass to kiss, trust me, been there-done that and I'm not doing it again.

It's like every place I've ever lived at was nothing but a boxed in nightmare, I might as well just said forward my mail to hell's front door. Once my friend Ayana came by the house to check me just to see what was good or whatever one day and of course Shawn had a major problem with that and had to threaten to cut her face up if she ever came back! Because of his ridiculous behavior I lost all the one-time friends I had and was left with no one to run to but drugs and alcohol when he got on his everyday slavery bullshit. To make matters worst any babysitter that I ever found big spender would tell them that he'd pay them fifty dollars a night to watch Tatiana and then when it came to pay he'd leave me to foot the bill when he knew damn well I couldn't. He just wanted to be an ass and make my life as miserable as possible.

After fucking with Shawn or should I say having a baby by him he fucked up my whole flow, trying to maintain being a stripper with him around was not happening. He's the worst, he'd complain, complain, complain all day long about guys being able to see me and then come to the club at night and stalk me. When he met me I was a stripper-duh what the fuck! You'd think I was the one with a split personality and selective memory the way he was getting at me, I mean all this was known, I didn't hide anything unlike him I kept it official.

So as time progressed I switched my hustle, I got my bartending license from New York Bartending School and did me on the night scene once again. I got my first job at Essence Bar and Lounge working three days a week making a thousand dollars a week for pouring drinks and socializing! Being the natural born Trinidadian hater he is Shawn couldn't stand the fact I didn't need him to support me financially anymore, I had my own money to do everything I wanted. I could afford to pay all my bills, a babysitter, stack the fridge up lovely and stay fly all at the same time with no strain, once again life was gravy until he figured out a way to fuck it up. I loved working at Essence because it never felt like I was at work cause I had all the good nights like karaoke, comedy and jazz so anytime I was there it was something popping! I could brush up my vocals on a karaoke night and laugh my ass off with the comedy shit and mellow out with the jazz vibe and get my mind right, I loved that shit.

It doesn't take a genius to figure out how I lost my job-you should know the drill by now. It started with my fucking low down and dirty hating ass baby father coming through starting arguments about nothing. Then one night he pops up with his friend, which should've been a sign because he never brings anyone with him when he's out stalking. When he comes to the bar I go get him a drink and tell him he has to pay his pending tab from the night before because that's the rule plus my manager was sitting right at the bar watching me. Mind you the night before he bought all his friends drinks and wasn't being generous at all-he was just trying to leave a high ass tab on me to cut my money short. That way I'd end up having to ask him for some money to do what I had to do so it could make him feel like I needed him again. I mean this wasn't the first time he did it and the manager being the hatter that she is knew what Shawn was up still let it go down! She even came to the bar and sat right next to Shawn to see if I was going to comply with my job orders. I was in a no win situation, she knew he was there to cause conflict and Shawn never gave a fuck so basically I was damned if I did or damned I didn't!

Everybody knows money wasn't shit to Shawn; he could've covered it if he wanted to but decided to flip so he could execute his well thought out plan as usual. First he starts talking that he aint paying shit! I would've let him slide but my manager was right there and I couldn't do it and the fucked up thing is he knew it but continued to go on with the he aint paying shit. Blowing the whole thing out of proportion his ignorant ass throws a fucking drink on me, so I busted him in right in his face with a glass and he busted me back in my head with a glass. So by this time we going back and forth as usual busting shit like we did at home until I started taking every fucking candle off the table and bombarding him with flying lit up candles! That shit aint even stop his possessed ass, he still wanted to beat on me some more so he came charging after me like maniac while I ran in the ladies room.

Surprisingly I never got fired, I just never went back because I was so embarrassed and ultimately it would only happen again, so what's the point? I was so depressed afterwards cause I was stuck, I gave up I just started doing whatever he said and got high and drunk and lived like a zombie in twenty four hour stupor. It was still like nothing I ever did was ever good enough for Shawn, long as I was depending on him, getting my ass whipped by him faithfully and being a sex slave-he was happy.

I'm sure there are a lot of housewives that don't work or pay rent and just take care of their kids and other domestic duties that don't have to go through the pain of abuse. There's no reason any woman should have to go through that, if a man feels like he has to hit a women he should just leave her alone. It got so bad I felt like I would've rather have nothing to my name, broke as fuck and be homeless before I continued to live my life with him! I had to do something and make an attempt at getting away from that evil mother fucker so I enrolled in G.E.D classes at Medgar Evans High School so at least I could salvage my sanity and try to make a change in my life. I figured something had to give sooner or later so I kept on trying and maintaining as much as I could. If I wasn't going to do it for me, I had to do it for my helpless child who was caught up in the middle of a disaster area that would ultimately put her mother in the crazy house. I swear on numerous occasions Shawn would tell me that's exactly where he would send me when he was finished with my ass-to the fucking crazy house! I told you his ass is evil, I started to pray, pray and pray!

In March I finally got a come up from a lawsuit I had from way back for a slip and fall accident and got hit off with about 22 thou! I hit Shawn with four to get him out my face and off my shit, bought me and icy piece and my daughter something's, paid my bills off and stacked the rest. Everything was popping for a minute, I went to Diddy's spot Justin's to get low for a minute because I needed to get away and blow some steam as usual. I came through door like I owned the spot with all eyes on me like I walked in that bitch wit Puffy beside me. I was rocking my blue and black fox, some sick ass bling and a crazy pair of Steve Maddens nobody was touching at the time and stepped over to the bar to grab me an apple martini. All of a sudden this big ass security guard comes and shuts the bar down, I was like aint that some shit-I just got here! I'm thinking to myself it's a Reynolds it just wasn't meant to be so I started putting my coat back on and was about to breeze when the security dude stepped to me and told me his name was Killa and I could stay and have a drink on him if I'd like. Of course I did, why wouldn't I, I was trying to get my drink on!

As I sat at the bar chilling with Killa and his boy I overheard him telling his man about a paid vacation in Miami he was about to go on the next morning. Since I needed a vacation I invited myself like, "Yo I was thinking about getting away, good, now I got somebody to go with." Just like that we settled it and from there it was on, I went home and packed my shit and thought about all the fun I was gonna have till I fell asleep. God knows I needed it! I'm telling you I was passed the fuck out, clothes on and everything, a bitch laaaiiid out! All that excitement and the thought if some peace and quiet in my life got to me but you better believe I was up the next morning and on my A-list baller shit. I hit Flatbush got fly, texted Killa I was leaving out at 7:30 that night and would meet him at the Crown Royal hotel on Collins Ave. and everything was a go.

M-i-a was heaven, four days of pina colodas and great sex ya digg! Nobody hit me, sniffed my ass, told me what to do or stressed me and I relished every moment of it you hear me. It's sad when normal shit like peace and tranquility becomes spectacular to you, I guess that just shows exactly how twisted my life really was back then. Besides the bikes we rented we barely left our room, we just went at it all damn day and night like we was down there on a porno shoot. It was so ironic talking to Killa because I found out we knew some of the same people, like Zab Judah for instance. Killa was like yo that's my man we tight and I'm like word get out of here, I been wanting to fuck him for a minute but every time we run into each other my stalking ass baby father be around cock blocking-n-shit! We just started laughing and fucking like a vacay away is supposed to be.

I can't even lie, straight up I was scared to go home, I knew Shawn would be looking for me and you know how he like to make scenes and I wasn't ready or in the mood for it. When I got to back to New York I was scared to see him so I had left my shit at this chick crib I thought had my back but really didn't. And the reason I say that is cause she had to be putting that nigga Shawn on to my where abouts. Come on … do you think it just happens to be a coincident that she knew I was going to Justin's and right when I'm chilling in VIP with Killa, Zab and Black Rob super stalker Shawn appears out of nowhere straight tripping!

Psycho Demon doesn't even park his fucking car he just jumps out and leaves his shit parked in the middle of the street! We're in the middle of Manhattan not some country ass town no one drives down with one traffic light in the whole fucking town-I should've never went shopping with that nigga! Why does he sit right next to me and in between Zab and start popping shit and acting like a little bitch talking about, "That's my baby mother son" and a whole bunch of other irrelevant bullshit! Straight cow-ass-bull-shit! He was beasting like I was his wife or something, I wasn't even his girl for real-at that point I was just his b.m. fall the fuck back, you live with another bitch named Janette! Okay he knows Zab from around the way and all but still fall the fuck back it wasn't even like that, if two people wanna fuck they're gonna fuck and it's nothing no one can do about it straight like that.

I should've told him Zab had a nice hand full of my ass standing right in front of him and see what he would've done ... come on, get real Zab knocks niggas out for a living so it wouldn't even be fair but on some real shit why not? He always wanna put his hands on me like I'm his equal, I should've let Zab knock him the fuck out early! Anyway me and Zab left Shawn walking around acting like an ass ruining everyone's vibe and went outside and blew it down.

While the cop had Shawn outside looking for a place to park his car, I was in this cut Killa used to take me when he wanted to get some privacy. This time when he took me, he took me on the elevator one flight down off to a room towards the left with a bunch of lockers I never seen before. I'm thinking the whole time he must be taking me out a different exit cause he already knows the situation and Justin's isn't the place for all that shit Shawn was getting ready to pull. But little did I know Killa was bout to keep it gullier then I imagined!

Killa pulled out this big ass machine gun looking type of burner and pulled that shit back like clack clack and I thought to myself yea I can really rock with this nigga! Talk about holding me down, Killa came up with a plan to get me out of there and everything, he came back upstairs with Zab, a female and a few dudes and told me he was gonna have the cops come escort me out and told me to meet him at his crib later-I was like bet so we did that shit.

I went back up stairs and talked to Shawn like it was nothing to play it cool, I told Shawn repeatedly I don't want to be you and his ass just kept acting like he didn't hear a word I said but I know he did, we were right next to each other. He continued to live in denial until the cops came and got me and I told him, "I don't want to be with him but he keeps trying to force me to", after they asked us what the problem was. I was telling the truth and everybody could see it so the cop was like aight come with me miss and with no hesitation I bounced. Shawn stood there like a bitch in the middle of the floor repeating "ayo that's my baby's mother" till the cop got tired of it and said, "well she's in my hands now what do you want to do about it?" Do you know that loser actual said "but that's my baby's mother" again as the cop put me into a cab! What a loose cannon, that policeman was like, "the minute you get a chance get an order of protection on him", it gotta be places he can get some help because that shit is deep. How do you stand there and keep telling a cop the same thing he already knows and you're obviously in the wrong? Psycho I swear.

I killed some time at C-Love's house for a while before I went to the Bronx and got back up with Killa and fucked him all night as usual, Killa was like, "Yo your baby's father is crazy!" He told me how he followed Zab all night making empty threats in VIP like a fucking groupie talking about, "yea nigga I'll end your career" and blah, blah, blah and a whole bunch of bullshit, he even followed that nigga back to his crib! Shawn was taking it to the extreme, if Zab would've hit him one good time that would've ended all that! That's why I love Zab cause he's a real ass nigga even though he likes to play the role like a lot of hood niggas who make it big, he don't little petty shit get to him. He could've been wired his jaw. I swear I love Zab so much that if he were ever to be like "yo China marry me" I'd do it with the quickness!

That was all Friday, the next day Saturday after all that shit went down the night before there was a big party jumping at the Roxy and I was back with my drink and my two step and being stalked by delusional baby's daddy ... again! I knew who the nobody ass snitch who was putting him on but I didn't give a fuck, I grabbed a bottle of Cris and hit the floor, fuck him and fuck her. It must have been like the stalkers reunion or convention that night cause one of his best friends baby moms was in the spot and she started keeping tabs too! Them niggas is and was losers for that shit, how you gonna be following me around like I'm ya child in a sandbox, it's a club, do you and get the fuck off my shit and find somebody to go home with, fucking lame ass niggas. Anyway I ended up meeting Funk Master Flex and passing him my math right in front of Shawn's face and all he did was stand there and watch me get my action lined up like the bitch that he really is. Even when Flex followed me to the parking lot where Shawn's whip was parked cause he knew something was up, Shawn still aint say shit-not a word! That nigga was quite like a house mouse in the p's looking for cheese, straight Fievel ass nigga for real. Flex was even like, "Mami what's wrong?" and I told him out right, "Nothing let me deal with this nigga then we'll get up" and that's exactly what it was till Flex wasn't in sight. The moment Flex bounced and slide off Shawn started punching me in my face, ripping my clothes off and macing me! It was one thing to hit me like a bitch but you wanna mace me like a pussy ass traffic cop? I was so feed up with his bullshit we went at it for a minute before he got the best of me and I ended up in the hospital.

They say that normally men who hit women are scared to fight men which I believe is partially true considering I didn't see him bark on Flex when he followed me to the parking lot or Zab when he saw us together, he wouldn't even act like he was gonna get at Flex or Zab but he had no problem bringing it to me? Yea he's pussy. I could never understand why a guy would hit a girl that he claims he wants to be with, unless he's a loser and feels like the only way he can keep her is if he scares her. Even with that eventually you'll turn the bitch into a killer and you'll be the one fucking running. I don't know how many times I thought about stabbing that nigga Shawn to death in his sleep, two wrongs don't make a right but I sure as hell thought about it … he's not worth me doing twenty-five to life. He's killed enough of my life, I'll be damned if he gets another portion, somebody's gotta be the bigger person in every situation and in this one unfortunately it was me.

About two days after Shawn busted my shit Flex called me on my cell and asked me to meet him in Manhattan so he picked me up from Justin's and we linked up. He took me to the Bronx to some spot where he keeps his cars and handles some type of business I assume, cause we went upstairs in an office where two tables and chairs were setup with a bunch of tires. I remember it was a little different then your average setup cause I almost bust my ass as soon as I came in there, because there's something like a floor but not a floor to the right of the office that's made of some gate like material! All I know is my heel got caught up in the bitch and I almost landed on my ass but I have balance like a cat so I was good!

Back on his Hot 97 shit Flex interviewed me like I was a guest on his fucking show! I'm thinking to myself my album aint dropping and I'm not in a movie so why are we playing twenty-one questions, when is he gonna stop this interview shit and get to fucking? When I told him I was bored with it and I wanted to know when we was gonna start fucking he found it to be o' so humorous but I was dead ass, I wanted to know! I could listen to the radio for all that, I just wanted to get it poppin fuck all the talking! After he told me to come over to him we got down to business …

He put my back towards him so my ass would be facing his dick and reached around me and started unzipping my zipper, since I didn't have panties on it was no problem for him to have easy access to my pussy and start rubbing my clit. I don't know how he did it but I loved it, he had my shit sooo wet it started running down the side of my legs, then bent me over the office table and started pumping and out of me real fast and hard! It was crazy cause his dick was so big I was in pain but at the same time I wanted it all, I never felt nothing like it in my life! I was like "stop-stop" and when he did I was like when I tell you to stop don't-keep going, lol. Although I was in pain, it felt so good, he came fucking me from the back but he still wasn't finish yet! He snatched my shoes off because he said he was into feet and loved the way mine looked and it got him even harder!

He laid an old sweater on the office floor and told me to lay on it and got down and fucked me again! Flex was really dropping bombs that night, I felt every inch of his good ass dick in me when he put his weight up on me and I rapped my legs around his waist so he could get all of my wet dripping pussy. Oh my God when he put my legs over my head and down over my chest and started beating my shit up I thought I was gonna pass the fuck out! I couldn't breathe the way he was digging in me, that nigga was taking every piece of my pussy and I wanted to give it to him all! My pussy was even tighter then the first time that we did it! It was like he never would stop, he just kept getting hard for me till the point I don't even remember stopping, all I know is I fell asleep on the table and he was knocked out in the chair! When he woke up he was like damn I gotta get home, so we got dressed and left the garage, went to Mc Donald's next door and breezed. He put me in a cab with two hundred cash and I was off to Brooklyn mesmerized.

7

Vacation Time

The more and more Shawn got on my fucking nerves the more I tried to stay gone, physically and mentally-he was killing in more ways then one. I had to do something to get away, I prayed a lot but still I needed to be in a different environment and since I was still sitting on paper I spent even more time in my home away from home. I went back down to Miami to help my boy Boo Blades promote his mixtape but truthfully I really did way more partying then anything.

Boo and I had a little history but by that time he and I were both past that, I was with my baby's father at the time so back then those emotions weren't going anywhere. Plus Blades had a bad habit of telling me he wanted to make me his bitch and I wasn't with it, I aint nobody's bitch! If anything I got bitches, you see how they act before and after they smell it, I keep 'em open like bodegas and Now and Laters in the hood, please me somebody's bitch-imagine that. Actually when I was supposed to be out promoting I ran into Zab again at Duvet but he was way too busy to chill and I wasn't about to chase him around any club in Florida or New York like a chicken with his head cut off. We travel the same circle, I knew I'd see him again, we've been doing it for years, we gave each other a kiss on the cheek and kept it moving simple as that. I bumped into Fabolous and ended up fucking one of his boys AB, he was supposed to get up with us but he never did, it didn't make a bit of difference to me because the highlight of my night was shaking Denzel Washington's hand. Me and AB fucked with each other hard for a minute after that but eventually lost contact. AB's a nut, he told me how he was telling Fab all about how he missed out and it was his lost, I guess he probably realizes now I aint "Plain Ol' Mary" like I told him when he asked me my name.

You know what's crazy, remember when I said I lost touched with AB for a minute ... well I ended up seeing him again back in Miami for Memorial Day at a club called Mansion. Not only that but the whole time I was fucking with Flex in N-Y, he never mentioned he would be spinning in any particular place and I never said exactly where I would be clubbing at when I hit Miami yet we all ended up at the same spot! It didn't make a bit of difference to me because he's married I'm single and I can do whatever the fuck I wanna do. Either way you look at everybody was at Mansion's that weekend from Jadakiss, D Block, Remy Ma, Fat Joe and Jay-Z and a bunch of other people, the shit was celebed the fuck out!

Okay random shit happens to me all the time but some how or another the club owner approaches me and ask me would I dance for the club-not on no strip shit-just dancing, so I agreed and next thing you know I'm on top of a podium dancing in front of about three thousand people strong. It was all good though cause I was having a ball and thinking nothing of it, the drinks just kept coming and I was doing me and letting everything in my head at the time go. I was in a zone in around all those people when I suddenly felt some big ass dude's hand tugging at my leg, I was thinking to myself "what the fuck does he want" but I aint say it, my look probably did, I really only said, "Yes?" Big man was like Flex told me to tell you his wife is here, I was like "okay", it wasn't like I was about to jump him on the stage or anything halfway related-I went home with somebody from D-Block that night, I was far from on it like that.

The next day guess who was ringing my jack talking about my wife's not gonna be at the club I'm playing at tonight come through and see me? Yup it was ya boy Flex, I wanted some dick and I knew he would more then deliver so I meet up with him like he instructed without an argument, we always got along anyway but I'm just saying-I didn't mind. I needed to get fucked royally, so I got to the club about ten and literally damn near ten minutes later Flex was asking me where I was at! By the time he found me in the back by the dj's both the first thing he did was grab a big chunk of my ass mad hard and tight, no "hey what's up" just squeezing! Flex's aggression and strong desire to fuck me turned me on so much I wanted to bang him out right then and there! I didn't have to wait to long to get what I came for he only played for about an hour and left.

Once we got out the back door four gorillas walked us over to a black SUV and he began to fondle my breast right there in the truck while his niggas chilled, he must've been horny and pressed for time cause he got right to the point and told me, "China we only have a little bit of time cause I have to catch my plane" and told the bodyguards, "I don't care I have to get apiece of that before I leave!" He obviously meant every word that he said because he had one of brolick body-guards take me to a where they staying one floor up from where his Flex's wife was waiting for him at. While me and the bodyguard rode the elevator he tried to make small talk asking me if he knew from Club Cheetahs, I recognized him too but I don't fuck the help so I was just like maybe and keep insisting it was me, whatever just lead me to where I need to be.

After waiting for about five minutes for Flex he came knocking at the door just as I was thinking to myself how much I couldn't wait to fuck him and how big his dick was is! Until I started fucking with Funk Master I thought that Aaron Hall was holding the biggest dick I ever had but I scratch that-it's Flex. When I let him in the door the first thing he did is go straight to the bathroom and change into his boxers and T-shirt, then for a brief moment we looked into each other's eyes and it was on! He grabbed me by the waist and turned me around so that my ass was directly facing his dick and wrapped his arm around me and slowly began running his hand down my stomach down to the front of my shorts and started to rubbing my throbbing clit. His strong hands moved my clit from side to side and all around until my shorts were completely soaking and wet!

I couldn't wait for him to put it in after I felt his hard dick pulsating against my ass as it was eager to indulge itself in my fat sweet and juicy wet pussy! Soon as he ran his fingers up and down the opening of my vagina and back up to my clit I could feel myself melting like butter pecan in a bowl left on the kitchen table with the heat on in the middle of August! After getting my pussy to the maximum point of saturation, he laid me on the edge of the bed and immediately after I touched the king sized pillow top I could feel cum run down my pussy to my ass-seriously it slid to the point it wet my anal. I was burning up inside as when he stood there looking at my butt ass naked body for a nice sensuous minute, I know he enjoyed the view of my legs cocked wide open and my breast bare and hard. I realized as he continued to massage my clit he was gonna make me beg him to put it in, I couldn't wait any longer even though I was already in ecstasy so I did, I was like, "Flex put it in papi, I need it now!"

I'm telling you Flex was really playing tough that night, he grabbed the head of his big, fat, long, and juicy dick and rubbed it from my clit down to the crack of my ass over and over again making me urn more for him to enter me! I know he could only take so much teasing himself so in a matter of seconds he put his dick right in the center of my whole and pushed it in nice and slow. Gradually he picked up the speed thrusting in and out of me hard and fluently, at one point all I could hear was my pussy popping! It felt so damn good I had to grab him by his shoulders and pull him close to me, I had to hold him tight to show him some love cause he was making it do what it do! About five minute's after all this quality lovemaking he pulled out me and poured every drop of his hot cum all over my clit. I enjoyed every minute we spent in that room but I was tight as hell cause

I knew there wouldn't be a round two cause he had to catch a flight! If I could've I would've flown him home myself after a couple more rounds.

After-matter fact my pussy's getting wet just talking about it! Hold up, hold up, hold up! I gotta go play with myself a minute I'll be right back!..... .I'm back! It felt that damn good, I don't know if I ever been that wet, my shit was soaked like the Atlantic Ocean. He told me I could stay there until tomorrow if I wanted but what for if I was gonna be there by myself. I just went back to my spot at the Catalina and drunk some Henny and daydreamed about his dick and played with myself some more. I remember thinking to myself damn I just fucked him in a room right over his wife's room ... I wonder if she could hear me moaning as loud as I yelled cause I damn sure did it loud and long enough! I didn't give a fuck if she heard me or not, it just turned me on more, it's funny how much sneaky shit can turn you on.

All good things must come to end right ... well when my off the chain vacation was over and I got back to hell's front door, Satin in the flesh was waiting for me. This time Shawn completely lost his mind, first he acted like everything was cool and there was no beef until the next day. After he came home from having a few drinks of God knows what he tried to grab my phone to start his shit-that wasn't about to be happening so he fucking grabs Tatiana's karaoke and beats me in the head with it! I kept going in and out of consciousness but luckily the 911 operator heard everything on speakerphone, she even heard him beating himself in the head. It was all for show though, cause when he realized the cops were coming he told me to suck it up cause if I didn't we were both going to jail. At that point I had enough and I didn't give a fuck, take me to jail. I'd rather go to jail then an early grave and if I didn't he would've surely killed me or would've died trying.

When the cops finally arrived they told both of us, "ya'll can stay in the house and act like it never happened or I'm taking both of ya'll to jail" ... I turned around and put both hands behind my back-take me to jail, my life is more important then him worrying about paper work-fuck that you taking me to jail! I spent two days locked up and decided I was out, as soon as I got out I took eight police reports out from under my couch and a few other things and called the domestic violence hotline for women and bounced. It was time to start a new life for me and Tatiana for good ...

8

Checked Into Heaven

I checked into the "Ivy House" in Harlem and tried harder then ever to maintain my sanity, I got away from Shawn but I still had to deal with a lot of bullshit living in a shelter. The setup wasn't bad considering what it could've been, the shelter was broken up into units and in each you unit you had a roommate but you still had your own room and a kitchen and bathroom you had to share with your roommate. The shelter also had a in-house daycare which made things a lot easier and it was always clean so that was cool, but I had to be in there by ten every night and that sucked especially being there in the summer time and you know how the summer get. I was tight but I made due, it was just one step to another. Although there were a lot of things about that shelter I could do without, I was glad I went because it allowed me to test into college and even better myself even further.

My roommate Shantay was a bitch, I couldn't stand her skinny ass, at first we were cool but we were total opposites so it was only a matter of time before me and her would get into it on a regular basis. Her conniving ass was probably the only one miserable in the whole place because everyone else was happy to get out of their situation but she didn't have one. She told me she lied about going through domestic violence and was only there to get an apartment through the shelter. If you ask me she's a dumb ass considering she was living out of state before she entered the shelter and wasn't even eligible for housing, you'd think she'd do her homework before signing her and her daughter in. Not to mention if anyone couldn't secure an apartment in three months you would be shipped off to a regular shelter then after that you were on your own.

You'd think Shantay would be on her grind trying to get out of there but she was more concerned with eating my food and socializing with everybody in the damn building trying to make friends so she could gather up a anti China Starr hating group. I could careless about the food cause even though I was in a shelter I was still living good or at least better then most, Shawn still gave me money and

I ate out all the time. I stayed eating at Mr. Chows having steaks, lobsters and BBQ's all the time, I wasn't on it like that, I didn't give a fuck but when that nerdy wanna be hood ass bitch wanted to act a fool one morning I showed her another side. I don't know what got into her but she came busting in my room six o'clock in the fucking morning like I was her child asking me for her daughter's sippy cup! Mind you I just bought her daughter two brand new cups a few days ago. It was too damn early to be yelling about some stupid shit with a stupid fucking bitch from New Jersey!

Since she rudely awakened me she got to hear my mouth, I went in the living room and was like, "Look my daughter is four years old what the fuck does she need with a fucking sippy cup and didn't I just buy you two new ones?" She was just looking for a reason to flip cause she just failed the test for college and I passed so she wanted to piss on my parade but I wasn't having it. I ignored her looser ass for a minute and sat at the kitchen table with Tatiana and fixed us some cereal and started eating when that retarded bitch decides she wants to yell at the top of her lungs and kick over one of the chairs that was sitting at the table. That was it that was the straw that broke the camels back, what if that chair would've hit Tatiana? Then what, I would've had no choice but fuck her up. I was already looking at the brand new knives I had just bought and she could see me looking at them the whole time, so she stood still for a minute after she pulled that stunt! I already wanted to fuck her up for numerous reasons anyway that would've just been another. After I told that frail bitch to kick me because chairs don't kick back she stood there with another dumb look, then I asked her how does your foot feel, lol.

Just like I figured she was all talk and no action and I wasn't in the mood to play the role of her anger management counselor so I called downstairs like, "you better come get this bitch before I kill her ass." Instead of telling her to come downstairs or coming to get her, the lady told me to come downstairs like I started the shit! Luckily thinking about everything else I had on the line I decided to use my better judgment and go downstairs and handle my business the correct way. Shantay was trying to take me down with her because she was going to be sent another shelter regardless. They shouldn't subject people to share rooms with people who don't have anything to loose with people who do cause it leaves to much room for the other person to be taken advantage of and cause an innocent person like me to be doing twenty five to life upstate right now, lol. But I had my own plans so yea I ate that shit and had to be the bigger person. That airhead loser eventually calmed down and from then on out I killed her with kindness instead of going back at her. I even paid for her to get her feet done, not because I was that nice but because I was tires of having to see them horrible monsters early in the morning while I was sitting at the kitchen table.

While she was busy trying way too hard to make my life miserable I was continuing to spend majority of my time in realtors looking for an apartment. The next day after about the tenth realtor I went to I finally found my apartment that same day! God I couldn't have planned it better, I never said a word about it to anybody I lived with and kept it moving and waited for my paper work to go through. If I would had told her she definitely would have tried to get me kicked out, cause beating on furniture was all she had to do before so if she just touch me lightly and I would've drug her by her nappy ass hair down to the first floor-five flights down! Which was what I had planned to do if she got the balls to be a real gangster and stop all the fucking talking and get down to the get down.

It got even better cause the tables started to turned on Shantay, one of the girls she initially became friends with to intimidate me was a big bitch that wanted to go upside what she had left of a head for borrowing money she couldn't come up with. I was laughing my mother fucking ass off! That girl started harassing her all the time and it wasn't nothing she could do about it, because one of the many rules of the boot camp slash shelter was nobody could borrow money from anyone else in the shelter or you'd get kicked out.

Before that girl was on her ass Shantay would be out in the hallway with her friends ranting and raving about dumb shit making noise all hours of the night, knowing I had to be in school the next day and focused. She aint care then but when home girl pressed her that bitch was playing hid and seek and that mother fucker! Well it only got better, me and that girl got cool and being that we booth from Brooklyn we shared the same attitudes towards Shantay and she soon learned the hard way, "we don't do no talking we get it poppin." Lol. Just to be spiteful I would be all in the hallway laughing and letting the girl taunt her by leaving the door open and letting her call her all types of bitches and telling her to come in the hallway. I used be cracking the fuck up but you know what? It's her own fault because if she if she didn't start nothing won't be nothing. What was that bitch crazy, she was in my mother fucking town and bitch, as we all well know, "I run New York!"

I finally got a much need brake one night when Shawn was unable to pick me up from my bartending job I had on Thursdays which was coincidently the only night I was able to stay out past ten and didn't have to be back at the shelter until six in the morning, so I took full advantage. It was like the "Starr's" were aligned that night in club Eugene's with DJ Carmelo on the one's and two's, Killa Cam, Jim Jones, Lil Weezy, that wanna be Marilyn Monroe bitch of rap Gloria Velez and myself China Starr were all in the building! It had been a while since I got a chance to really get down and party like I wanted to being that I was always cooped up in that shelter ... I couldn't even have company in that mother fucker-it was just me, my daughter and my funky ass roommate.

Well I spotted Gloria chilling with her back towards me and I crept up on her and whispered in her ear, "what up Peebles" to let her know yea chick I know ya ass before "Big Pimpin" so don't forget who's whose protégée. She turned around like "oh what up China" and went on to say outlandish shit about bitches in New York don't be getting no money and all that-how she figured that when we the home of the hustle I don't know? But I could careless I wasn't there for all that, I was there to enjoy myself and have a good time, I was gonna play it nice and steal her shyne as usual. I mean I didn't have to try, I just did, I'm a Starr it happens everywhere I go. Point and case, some dude she was with started taking mad pictures, I mean mad pictures of me and her and at first she was cool with it until he told her to slide so he could get a few of just me. Siiiicccckkk! Oh' shit she was bluer then a Yankee fitted! One of the dudes's passed me a glass of Grey Goose and while I was getting my drink on, all of a sudden the shit jumped off!

Cam and Jimmy got into some beef and Dipset pounded the living shit out some niggas, them dudes got their fronts knocked out and white tees blood burgundy dyed, what the fuck was they thinking? They should've known better to fuck with the D-I-P boys, lol. Everybody bounced and ran off and did they own thing after that but me and Gloria was standing there like the party must still go on, let's get it! So on our way to the dj booth we talked about this and that and I mentioned I rapped and the notorious blonde biting h-o-e asked like she aint know; talking bout "word?" Like I wasn't the only one in the dressing room back in the day rhyming before we got on the stage, that bitch kills me with Hollywood shit, nigga I know you, you did everything but come out my pussy!

You know she played herself right? Why she pick up the mic and started spitting bout a bunch of nothing, I give it to her she said a few things to make the crowd say a few oh's and aw's but nothing serious-I did that. She passed me the mic hesitantly cause she knew-like I said-I get in that ass. I was bout to shut her down lyrically cause it's obvious I could kick her ass and it really wouldn't get me anywhere so I spit some slick shit something bout ... "this hoe's name is Glo/ she's a wanna be J-Lo/but is J-Lo from Florida nooooooo." I showed her how real NY chick's get down, we stay fly from head to toe and when I was done with her she was just standing there on the stage looking assed out and not even trying to touch the mic a second time, so I passed it back to Camelo and let him rock. The next time I saw Carmelo was in Club Eugene's again and he was like "China

Starr's in the building" and it shocked the shit out of me because it let me know that he was really listening to my rhymes that night, and had enough respect for me to mention my name.

You know word travels and I heard how she had a lot to say about me fucking her baby's daddy but never once that night did she mention it, cause if she did I would have told her how I sat all on his fucking face for hours, she really didn't want to get her fucking feelings hurt. All she could talk about was the fight she had with Remy Ma minus the details of her getting her ass whipped-it was official, Flex confirmed it. I mean it doesn't take much thought to figure Remy would fuck her up lyrically or in the streets just the same as I would and she still stuntin? Matter fact I even heard she got her ass kicked by that chick from Florida that be in all them uncut videos that had a fight with Foxy, I can't remember her name though cause she was a ugly ass nobody. Anyway I figure she took the "if you can't beat them, join them" approach because after I killed her and I walked off she followed me back to where I was at and started dancing on me but even that aint work cause some dude I was already dancing with was like, "damn she can't wait her turn." I was laughing my ass off and I guess she sensed she was out of pocket and slid off never to be seen or heard from again that night.

Cam'ron came back minus Jim Jones but Weezy was with him and we all ended up chilling in a secluded section, getting high and drunk. I tried to get some love on the L Cam was blazing but he was acting stingy and aint wanna pass it but when he bought eight bottles of Cristal and I passed my cup he filled it to the rim! I guess he's only particular with his weed, I didn't give a fuck I smoked with Wayne he was cool. I pretty much Debo-ed his Dutch but he didn't seem to care until I blew this chick a shotty, he grabbed the bud from shorty and gave it back to me and by time he actually got it back it was just about a roach. That nigga Wayne just looked and said, "damn" and laughed. Over all I had a good time and the night was getting late and I wasn't trying to fuck up curfew and a bunch of them niggas was acting anti-social so I bounced without saying a word. I ran circles around everyone that night.

I didn't need to get into any unnecessary trouble especially with my insensitive advocate Jacky, nobody could stand her, she was a mean ass miserable bitch. I hated going to those counseling sessions every week, I remember the one time I decided to go out on a limb and discuss the time I was abused and suffocated by my babysitter when I was six, she started laughing at me in a room full of strangers! I couldn't believe she fucking did that to me, I cried for weeks behind that, do you know how much it took for me to share that with complete strangers? Words can't even tell you the pain I felt, I wanted to break that heartless bitch's face in three pieces and fry it! And she's a fucking consoler? Even though that hurt, I could deal with that but to make matters worst she knew I could only spend three months there so you'd figure she'd do her job on the paper work tip but no. Two weeks after I turned in my papers and went to her office to see what's good, she told me she hadn't processed them yet! What the fuck was she getting paid for?

I just prayed for God to give me strength to overcome the barriers that were being placed in front of me and worked my way around it, it was no way I could do it on my own. Them haters was on me but September came and I went ... I moved right on to my apartment and floated on out of there like George Jefferson in his three piece suit! I looked at my daughter and like Lil Weezy would say I told Tatiana, "We outta here Baby!"

Before I left I had a few things to address like Shantay's scrawny ass, I told her at one point if I ever catch her in the street after I get out this shelter I would whip her ass and I meant it. But then I turned around and said, "when you get settled in the "next shelter" you make sure you call me if you need anything" to be extra, lol. Besides an apartment and the opportunity to go to college and get away from Shawn I got a chance to make up for the time I lost with Tatiana, that I lost spending at Chris's hot ass house getting high but that was all behind me ... I was free.

9

Free To Do Me

Now that I was I settled in my new place in the Bronx and Shawn was out of the picture far as being around and harassing me in his free time, I was able to live like the true Scorpio that I am. The whole time I was in the shelter I was still seeing Funk Master Flex, Killa time-to-time and dating Super Zab Juda.

After years of close encounters missed opportunities and pent up sexual energy me and Zab finally linked up at club Show in Manhattan, Justin's was dead and hot as hell cause Shawn more then blew that spot up. Show was perfect for us anyway because you couldn't get in unless you were on the guess list or was a celebrity and since Shawn was neither it was always a go. Killa was at Show that night and peeped me and Zab sliding off to the bathroom which I could tell made him a little mad because he really liked me and we had a good thing going so I can understand. But this thing with me and Zab was meant to be, Zab and I had been playing cat and mouse with each other since I was about eighteen and it was easily at least seven years later and we still hadn't fucked so something had to give.

Even though Killa wasn't too thrilled about me and Zab bout to jump off he surely invited himself along, he even gave us some E that all three of us took at the same time. It was funny seeing Zab's expression and watching him get mad when I was giving Killa head because he felt I wasn't paying him enough attention. I know Zab wanted me all to himself but he should've understood me and Killa already had a sexual vibe so he was the outsider if anything, I know Killa was in his ear bragging how he fucked me and how I had that good grade-a shit niggas fein for. While we in the stall and I'm going back and forth between Killa and Zab buffing them off, every time it was Zab's turn he kept beasting and acting extra thirsty like he never got his dick sucked before. He was way too excited and over doing it to the point he was trying to choke me with his dick, I threw up on his shit and he didn't even care, ex and all, and he still was into it! Too bad for him because after I threw up some of that ex it brought me to my senses and I was like I'm finished and neither one of them got bust!

There were some groupie ass niggas standing there chanting "go Zab, go Zab" as we left the bathroom like I gave a fuck, I didn't care what they said cause I wanted him in my mouth, my pussy, my ass-and wherever he wanted it. If it meant going to a club bathroom so be it, I obviously wasn't the only one sucking his dick that night, and they talk about women. Nobody made me do anything I aint wanna do, I told Killa before I wanted to fuck him and Zab at the same time and I would've been did it if Shawn wasn't always hating, if he could pay for pussy why couldn't I get mine for free? While we were in there, Killa brought it up to, talking about, "I see your wish came true cause you got both of us now", not really but close enough, I wanted to do it in different setting so we could really get it in. Anyway when we left the bathroom Zab started whispering in my ear, "China I've been wanting you so long, I want some of that good ass pussy I've been hearing about" and I was thinking to myself, "yea and I'm dying to give it to you too!"

Since Show it was a wrap, Zab was constantly trying to get at me and when I say he couldn't get enough of me he really couldn't and that's way before we fucked! I don't know why but for some reason I made him wait a little, I can't remember why but I did. He used to go to parties have a thousand bitches on him willing to do whatever the fuck he wanted at a drop of a dime, a wife at home and still call me asking me what I'm doing and can he come see me and fuck me and blah, blah, blah, he even threw his money out there. Zab aint have to do all that because it wasn't about money with me and him, we clicked, if I wasn't with Flex I was with Zab and vice versa, that's just how it was back then. I was officially Zab's BK chick cause every time he was in the hood my jack was popping, I never really had to use his number cause he always called me. I was like damn this nigga must be open giving me his numbers when he's married with children and everything, I guess if you want something bad enough you gotta get it. He was persistent in try to make me his side chick regardless of Shawn and Flex or anybody else, he couldn't give two fucks long as I was his he was good.

For some reason Zab was extremely infatuated with my ass-seriously. Every time he saw me in a club he had to rub my ass, touch my pussy and grab my titty's and whenever we had phone sex while he was on the road it was my ass this, my ass that, I wanna cum on ya ass, my ass, my ass, my ass. I should've got my salad tossed as much as he mentioned my ass, he used to love for me to talk dirty to him and let him call me his little bitch while he jerked off and yelled out

"China-China" while I'd play with my favorite vibrator. And you already know with the profession he's in he has quick hands so I aint gotta tell you he bust fast every time he did it, lol, if you saw him in the ring you can just imagine, lmfao. With celebrities always on the road all the time phone sex is the next best thing, I say whatever floats ya boat but I'm sure after awhile it gets old that's why they always tried to get me to go somewhere convenient for them every chance they got.

I swear Flex and Zab killed me always talking about let me put you up here or there like I was a fucking doll or something, like you can just put me where ever you want and I'll be there when you get back to me after you're done doing God knows what. Fucking men with money. Flex was trying to pull a power move trying to convince me to move to one of his cribs in Detroit and get a nanny for Tatiana so I'd be able to travel with him and live a fairy tale. I don't know how he thought that was going to work, really what the fuck would I want to move to Detroit for, Florida maybe but Detroit? That shit absolutely didn't make any sense since I had my own place and I was in college, why would I go, was I just supposed to switch up my whole program for him when I was just a piece of ass to him? Yea right, you can just pick me like you been doing and drop a bomb to that-thank you. Niggas get it twisted, just cause I might fuck with you and people know your name that doesn't mean I'm gonna play myself to be with you, I got fans too. Then here goes Zab talking out his ass, "I wanna put you up somewhere but your daughter has to go with her dad", yes he really did tell me that as if it were ever ganna happen, anybody who wants to deal with China better know my baby comes first and nothing in between. I love Zab but I'm sorry that would never happen for him or anybody else.

Dealing with a bunch of guys who've obtained some level of celebrity whether in the hood or in the industry I've noticed they tend to be on some other shit, doing shit they probably wouldn't do if they didn't have bread or had a name. For instance Cuban Lynx the rapper who was down with Fat Joe, Big Pun and the Terror Squad, I don't know what it is he does now but back in 2002 I bumped into him when I was a dancer at Sue's Rendezvous and it wasn't a good look. All I remember is popping an E pill before he came in and later drinking a few glasses of champagne at a table with him and then waking up in his house! No, he's the one wilding, people told me they saw him "carry" me out the club so that means I didn't leave on my own or was even aware I was going anywhere. Like I said I don't remember exactly what happened but I do know I had my period and I had a tampon in me when I was at the club but when I woke up at that rapist house I didn't have shit in me and when I went in the bathroom the next morning to check myself I saw a bunch of condom wrappers in the garbage so what do you think happened? I was at least thankful I wasn't tied to anything on top of that bunk bed, don't ask me, I don't know what I was doing up there. What the fuck is a grown man doing with a bunk bed anyway? The first thing I did when I saw him was ask him did anybody have sex with me and he just kept watching TV and said, "No, nobody touched you."

I didn't know whether to cry or whip his ass so I did neither, I just went home and smoked a blunt and charged it to the game. God don't like ugly and I saw his ass again, about three years later he was performing one of his songs nobody knows and I jumped on the stage and sung all over it and told him back in the VIP, "Listen the next time you wanna have sex with someone make sure that the other person is aware of it." Do you know his sick pussy stealing ass stood there with a blank look like I aint say a word! I can't say I was all that surprised because I heard he does shit like that all the time so he was probably used to it. That's probably how his face got fucked up in the first place, I hope somebody fucks his face up again soon, fucking rapist. Somebody should rape his ass, and to top it off that thirsty bastard actually had the nerve to tell me I was playing him close! Can you believe that shit? A rapist telling me I'm playing him close. That's what I mean, you get a little fame-and in his case I do mean a little fame and let it go to your head!

True I'd rather date a dude with gwop over a broke nigga any day but come on, step ya game up. Killa used to act funny and say little slick sarcastic shit when he'd see Flex come get me from Justin's in his red Lamb or even his down low po-po whip like "go Flex it up", I aint give a fuck-whatever he was catching a cab so "go yellow it up." Lol. Fucking jealous ass, can I live? Somebody always wanna rain on my parade, I don't hate I just let it be. I didn't tell Flex he should leave his wife when he would keep telling me they were having problems, I didn't give a fuck, it was obvious he was fucking me more then his wife! I never had a direct number to contact him at, only some number that didn't ring and only prompted you to leave a message and that was it, so if he didn't call me we couldn't hook up and we linked up all the time, so he didn't have to tell me shit far as I'm concerned.

After a year of steady fucking Flex was the one who wanted to go raw, it wasn't even something we discussed because it wasn't necessary from the beginning we always used a condom. One night when we was bout to get it on in the Bronx at this hotel we used to creep at, I was bent over and he started rubbing the head of his dick on my clit and was like feel my dick, then I realized he aint have a rubber on and then before I can say anything he was stroking in me hard-body! It felt like he was even bigger and harder without a condom and I loved it even more, especially since I was able to feel all of him, even his veins.

Truthfully although I dated Zab Judah and Funk Master Flex both for about a good two years I knew it wasn't a future in neither relationship other then the given: a good time. Both were married and had invested time and money with their wives, it was no room for me in the big picture so I played my part and took it for what it was worth, at best I could've been what ... a well paid mistress? Don't get it twisted even though I got mad love for both of them, I couldn't be neither one of them knowing how they really get down. How could I settle down with someone I know isn't capable of being monogamous? Sure all men cheat but I'd be a fool not to think it wouldn't happen to me considering the terms on which we were running, Flex was fucking me like my pussy was going out of style and Zab was in my ass more then my thong at Cherry's and both of them been married for years so why would I ever commit to either of them? I solemnly swear to enjoy myself and nothing else.

For a couple of years I felt like "I Love New York" between Shawn, Flex and Zab tryna claim me. Shawn had the inside advantage over them because we had a child together so he always had a reason to be somewhere in the picture even though at no point did I consider being with him. More or less he was just around fucking it up for everybody else-mainly me. I don't care who it was he would find away to throw salt in the game, one year we was at Mars 2112 for Baby's birthday party and Baby wanted to holla at me and once again my annoying ass shadow utters his favorite words to Baby's bodyguard, "that's my baby's mother." I whish he would just give it a rest, what the fuck! I bet you if you ever run into him he'll tell you I'm his baby's moms too, I didn't see his point cause Baby still got at me anyway. Zab was at Mar's that night too with his b.m. and wilding just the same, he sent Shawn off to get a bottle of Moet for us to drink and soon as he dipped Zab slide right next to me and asked me for my number right in front of his baby's moms! It didn't make a difference if she was standing there or sitting on the other side of me, I wrote it down and past to him like she wasn't even there, I know she was tight right along with Shawn when he figured it out. It just wasn't Shawn's night ... cause later on after we left the club to get a late dinner we ran into Baby and the minute he walked away Baby motioned he wanted to talk to me and I did. We only had time to kick it for a minute because Shawn came storming out the bathroom pouting and yelling he's ready to go and cut our conversation short.

Even though he gets on every last one of my fucking nerves and I wish he would just go somewhere and find someone else to stalk and harass, I could feel his pain. I mean I would be a little intimated if Laila Ali was stalking my baby's daddy, shit you aint winning that fight, lol. Maybe he'd handle it better if I was dealing with average everyday guys instead of celebrities but I doubt it, he has too much hate in his blood. He's never gotten over or accepted the fact I will never be his, he had his chance and blew it, tough luck I'm gone-see me with my money in hand.

I have so many memories in 2112, a lot of shit popped of for me in there, around the end of the year Zab had a birthday party at Mars and I hadn't really decided whether or not I was gonna leave with the birthday boy or with the Funk Master. I was gonna rock with however I seen first but I was leaning more so towards Flex for obvious reasons but I never ended up leaving with either one of them cause I never saw them! But it was a memorable night for me nonetheless, and I can't tell you what it is about Hot 97 and their dj's but I keep ending up running into one of Funk Master Flex's best friends, Bobby Trends.

It started off real innocent, I was dancing with a few guys including Zab's brother you know just to pass time and having a good time nothing serious, you know just feeling the vibe. When some random guy approaches me and tells me some guy wants to see me and I'm like "who" and he says "Bobby Trends from Hot 97", and I'm like oh he must be calling me for Flex let me go see what's good. Well I went over there and started to dance with him and see what he was talking about, and his dick got hard almost immediately! I found that shit mad funny cause all I was doing was dancing with him and I already could feel his shit coming out his pants but two Apple Martini's later I was horny as hell and ready to pop. By that time it was already towards the end of the night and I hadn't seen or heard from who I was checking for and he was like, "I'm about to leave, yo go get your coat and I'll meet you up front" so I was like okay we could do that. I noticed Booby constantly maintained a safe little distance from me while I was getting my coat, which told me "yea, he must be married too", it was a sign but just as fast as I thought about it, the thought left my mind and was out.

We had to wait a little while before we pulled of because he had to wait to get all his records from the club so in the mean time we listened to an underground cd I had. It was a little something I did rapping and singing over different tracks by a few different artist or whatever and I saw him nodding his head feeling it. He told me he liked it but I knew some how he'd end up like my good ass pussy even more, it never fails, niggas is so predictable. We went to go drop off his records, when I realized I've been here before. Do you know at first this dude tried taking me to this spot me and Flex used to get it on all that time, I was like, "ayo this is me and flex's spot this is aint gonna work, we gonna have to go somewhere else."

He knew I fucked with Flex but he still aint believe me until I explained to him exactly what the inside of the spot looked like and everything, then his ass was like "wow." But it really didn't make that big a difference to him cause he still wanted to fuck me anyway!

Bobby ended up talking me to some down low shit; it wasn't nothing expensive or anything worth bragging about just a spot to creep at for real. Once I came out the bathroom in my bra and panties he was rock hard and loving every minute of it. The four play wasn't that in depth, pretty much I laid on the bed and he rubbed my clit till I got horny and wet and after a few minutes I turned over and let him hit from the back. The more he watched his self fuck me in the mirror the harder he went, it was cool with me cause the harder he went the closer I got to cumin and eventually we did at the same time.

I'm telling you that nut wasn't worth all the bullshit I had to listen to after that he kept telling me a bunch of shit about his wife like I cared or needed to know. Do I give a fuck his wife always wanted to go on vacation and he couldn't take no more-nooo. He even told me, "I wish I could just lay down with you all day, but my wife would be looking for me" I didn't want him to go on and on so I was just like yea me too, only because I was tired and didn't feel like getting dressed yet-you know how that go. He aint kill nothing it was just late, the sex was at best aight, nothing worth mentioning other then he was Flex's boy and one week later me and Flex ended up at the same hotel! I told Flex what a coincidence out loud by accident when we walked in and he was like what's a coincidence and I just played it off like "nothing" I couldn't tell him! I was nervous as hell, and besides I couldn't get enough of him cause his dick game was official. I'm sorry but I wouldn't fuck that up for Bobby's ass and nobody else, shhiiiittt do I look crazy, lol.

10

When One Door Closes Another Opens

In November 2006 I decided to go to Miss Jones's birthday party at LQ's in Manhattan to celebrate a little because my birthday's the same month and it couldn't be better because that night set everything off for me. I saw Zab in passing earlier in the club along with Jonsey and figured Zab was upstairs in VIP mingling so I decided to go holler at him and see what was going on with the celeb's and others in the spot. I figured me and Zab had a history together so the least he could do was get me in cause I wasn't about to be paying or begging nobody to get through. So I fixed my tah-tah's and get'em in place and went right up top and just outside the entrance where I could see everything and everybody coming and going in order to make eye contact to with him to get in. Fuck all that yelling and putting myself out there like I was a stalker like Shawn.

Of course it worked, after we caught glances and I gave him the signal I was in, even though some dick head bodyguard wanted to act like an asshole telling Zab, "it's too busy up here there's not enough room up here!" Like it was really packed to that extent, but whatever fuck him because I still got in because another security guard recognized me from hanging out at Justin's told him, "ayo just let the girl up it's too hot right now!" I mean God, why does somebody who's never in control of anything at all always wants to be abuse their little bit of power the minute they get some? You know his hating ass still had the nerves to turn around and ask Zab are you sure! Fucking assholes.

Once I made my way pass Mr. Top Flight Security I found a spot to play the cut and still chill with Zab and everything was going good, when five minutes later a guy by the name of Kurt walks up and starts asking me a million and one questions. I was in a good mood and didn't mind because I was only going to tell him what I wanted him to know regardless of what he asked me. Kurt just came with it, "Who are you and who you trying to bag?" Since With my favorite drink that year, Patron with salt and lemon I gave him something his nosey ass wasn't expecting, "Trying to bag somebody, nah, I'm here to see Flex I thought he was going to be up here, I wanted to fuck him and bad too!" Yo you should've seen his face, he was like "how'd you get up here" and after I told him because I know Zab Judah he was like word you sound like you got an interesting life let me get your number so we can talk about it. I was like aight, after all he runs Datzwhatzup.net and I figured what could it hurt and really it couldn't.

A month later Kurt called me like he said he would and told me he was interested in doing an interview with me about all the celebrities I've been with. I was like "wow, let me get back to you I gotta think about it", I didn't know if I wanted to be involved with something like that but guess what? I thought about it and I did, it wasn't like I was exploiting anybody or getting a name off the people I been with like some hoes, I was talking about my life I just happen to know celebrities. I live in New York, I'm sexy and I party, I'm bound to meet people I don't have to chase nobody for action-I'm the life of the party so don't get it twisted. For legal reasons we were unable to disclose the names of the celeb's I talked about so we gave them nicknames instead, it was a good interview. The overall interview lasted over an hour over the phone and got me so horny reminiscing, especially when I got to Funk Master Flex and Aaron Hall, the rest of 'em were aight but them two, you already know! I kid you not, I told the guy interviewing me I was going to play with my vibrator the minute I got home and that's exactly what I did. All I can remember about that session is busting to Flex's name, I came so damn hard that night I think his wife must have felt it!

After the Datzwhatzup.net interview things just started clicking, not that long after the interview posted I got a call from one of Kurt's people telling me someone named Alissa was interested in me doing the Dr. Keith Ablow Show on Fox 5. That's the crazy thing about interviews and entertainment-you never know who sees you or who's out there watching so you always gotta be on point. Any moment could be a turning point so I'm glad I'm always prepared because it was nothing for me to milk my new chain of events. I didn't go all in with the Dr. Keith Ablow Show immediately because I hadn't heard much about him so I got online and did my homework before I got amped as hell. Once I found out the show was official and everything was legit I called Alissa back later that night and told her I was interested in doing the show. Even though Alissa told me straight up the topic of the show would be "groupies and females exploiting their secret lives with celebrities", which I feel I am neither-I agreed. I see an opportunity as an opportunity, call me whatever you like but I am not dumb. I've been on TV countless times before so I wasn't pressed or looking for my fifteen minutes of fame, I was out to get it and spread my name ya digg.

I was booked to shoot the show on December 21st in Rockefeller Center so I asked my boy Vaughn from Allthaclubz.com to come with me to keep me company before the tapping. I met Vaughn through Myspace but prior to that he'd already taken pictures of me at Miss Jones's birthday party so we actually met then but we really got to know each other online, I'm telling you you'd be surprised who'd you meet on Myspace-everybody's on it. The first time we hooked up was at Essence Bar on Atlantic and Troy in Bed Stuy when he picked me and my girl Eb up for a double date. I wasn't trying to chill there for obvious reasons so we left there and went to the Lenox Lounge on a 125th and got our drink on and just kicked it. On the way over there, I was mad, because we were supposed to go to a club in Manhattan, but all of a sudden my i.d was missing. I'm not going to lie, I thought that she had taken it, because she didn't have hers so I figured she had taken mines on some, "if I can't go to the club, you can't go shit." I was pissed off and started to speak out loud in the car saying to her, "Bitches be hating and they need to get their shit together" and et cetera, et cetera, et cetera. I didn't give a fuck if we was going to fight, but Eb probably was like this bitch is drunk so let me slide and she did. She told Vaughn to pull over the car and let her out, I didn't care either cause I was mad anyway. Besides she wasn't feeling his friend anyway.

We went to a bar instead and I was on my Patron like usual and he was drinking some Heineken beer when we went to the juke box and some Alicia Keys came on and he was like "yo my dick is hard" all out the blue, so I told him like Jay-Z, "oh yeah, well show me see what you got!" I'll give to him, Vaughn's not a fronter he pulled out his fat ass dick with no hesitation and I began to suck it right then and there at the bar! There were plenty of people in the club but everyone was in their own little world and nobody was paying us any attention so why not! We were getting it in until his loud mouth ass friend yelled "Ayo what ya'll doing over there" mad fucking loud! He spoiled the whole shit, he was from some other state so he wasn't used to how real NY chicks get down, that shit was too much for his ass, lol.

We rode in his black Caddie back to my house and got it poppin, while his friend sat in the living room; which didn't matter because we left the door open so he could hear everything. After that I sent him on his way, and slept like a baby that night. That guy had some serious pipe game, lol. The next day the 20th, I told Vaughn to come to my house that night so that he wouldn't miss the ride to the show, because they were to pick me up at seven o'clock in the morning sharp! I had to be in hair and make-up by eight! I was so nervous the night before I told Vaughn I needed my beauty sleep so we didn't' have any sex that night. We could barely sleep either. The transportation was on time, so we got to the studio early I was prepared and had time to relax before we started because going up there rushed and aggravated would have been a bad look. It's never good to do business when your emotions are not intact because you never want to kill something early. You never know what might happen down the road. Once we got through security and met the producer we were escorted to a guest room to unwind and have a little breakfast before I was scheduled to go on. Vaughn's nosey ass noticed a cue card and picked it up and started reading it then we found out Nas's baby's mother was going to be on the show too.

I wasn't hungry just eager to get in front of the cameras and speak my piece and introduce the world to China Starr so breakfast was just prolonging it far as I was concerned so I just tried to be patient. After eating and sitting in that damn room so long with all those mirrors exposing so many different angles our minds started drifting and before you know it we was in their feeling each other up! All that touching only lasted but for so long because we both grown, and being the freak he is Vaughn pulled out his fat dick once again for me to suck and since I aint never scared I began to put the head in my mouth. After I licked it a little I tried to put it all in but I couldn't get my mouth all the way around it because it was too fat, I think it grew! Lol.

I stopped messing with Vaughn's crazy ass to do makeup, and I was supposed to get my hair done while I was there but my shit was already laced so it was no need for that! Just do my make up please, lol. Vaughn tried to come in and take some pictures of me before my makeup was complete but I wasn't feeling him on that, because to me that seems like a set up for a fucked up picture. Trust me I don't look horrible without makeup but I'd just rather take the "after" pictures rather then "before", you won't have me looking caught off guard in magazine or online-fuck that.

Nas's baby mom's Carmen was on the show promoting her book "No Secrets" and talking a bunch of bullshit like she's not a groupie because she was dating all of the celebrities she's been with before they became famous! Imagine that, when has Jay-Z ever been on the come up? That bitch must be stupid he had a little fame before he dropped "Reasonable Doubt." I don't know how Jay was hitting that in the first place, she's ugly as hell with big baggy eyes and a fucked up stomach. When the staff was fixing her mic and her shirt came up you could see all of her nasty ass stretch marks, I almost threw up! I felt like I was drinking Henny on an empty stomach, I don't know how his dick even got hard. Say what you want about Nas but he definitely upgraded himself when he married Kelis, lol. That's how the game should be, when niggas date me they upgrade themselves all the time, they can never loose.

When the show was filming they had to stop for a few minutes and take two because Dr. Keith Ablow was like, "China's so cute I forgot what I had wanted to ask her!" After Dr. Ablow got it together he asked me were the celeb's I was having sex with married and I told him the truth. So when he asked me if I cared, I told him, "No I don't care, I'm single and I'm not married so I don't feel like I'm doing anything wrong. I'm just living my life and China Starr's going to be true to herself all day every day!" It was no need to front, I didn't give a fuck and neither did they if they did they would've never been around in the first place. I kept it real with Flex and told him I was going on the show before I did and he knew what I was going to say, he wasn't surprised. The only thing that got to Flex was when he asked me to name a few names and I got to Bobby Trends. He didn't care about Zab Judah, Ed Lover or anybody else and he been knew about Aaron Hall years ago, it was just Bobby Trends he was pissed about, the weakest mother fucker! I knew I shouldn't have fucked with him that night, it was a waste all the way around. Flex was pissed like I never seen him before, he just kept saying, "Not Bobby! Bobby! Are you serious!" Eventually he got over the initial shock of me and his boy getting it on and asked me was it before or after ma and him began seeing each other, I felt so bad when I told him it was after because he just went silent and wouldn't say nothing … I could tell he was disappointed.

After the show was wrapped up me and the girls took pictures and said our goodbyes and went our separate ways, Vaughn and I on the other hand went back to my crib and got it popping! Between what we did in the waiting room and all that talk about sex and the show bringing up old memories I was in heat in no time. Soon as we got in the door it was on! I'll never forget that day from beginning to end.

Since the Datzwhatzup.net interview I started wondering how I could turn my story into something bigger and the minute I finished the Dr. Keith Ablow show on national television I knew just how I would do it and got busy. No one enjoys spreading gossip more then Wendy Williams and it's no secret Wendy's the queen of that shit so I had to get to her! Coincidently sometime in early January before the show aired on Fox, I checked my yahoo account and I had a email promoting Wendy Williams was going to be at club Eugene's that same night. I couldn't ask for better timing I'm sure, it was like everything was just supposed to happen to me the way it did. I didn't know exactly what I was going to say to her when I get there, but I eventually shook everything out my head and realized all I had to do was tell her what I was up to and real recognizes real and she was either going to be with it or not. I was still gonna be China and I would just have to find another avenue.

I arrived at Eugene's about midnight or a little after and the line was long as Flatbush but I wasn't pressed, I knew I was going to get in, I always do, lol. I decided to lay low at the bar on the main level after I spoke with Kurt and took a few pictures and low and behold Wendy Williams walks right in. I had been chilling with celebrities before so I knew where they were going to seat her when she arrived. So I got my drink and two stepped my way back to the area where I knew she was going to be. Then boom, she plants herself right next to me, boy I tell you God has been good to me, he set me up and all I had to do was finish the rest. I went right into my master plan, after we established eye contact I told her she looked fabulous, which she did, and she said the same to me and invited me to a glass of champagne with her and husband Kev. So as we began to drink I told her I was on the Dr. Keith Ablow Show with Nas's baby moms and I was airing it out on several different celebrities myself. Once I told her the names of the guys I discussed she began to show a little interest and asked when the show aired. Unfortunately back then I didn't have a date because the show's producers hadn't given me a specific time, all I knew was it was going to be sometime in January so I had to tell her, "I'll keep you posted."

Wendy and I didn't exchange numbers but I knew just how to reach her-Myspace! I knew she had to have a page and when I found it I sent her over the interview I did with Datzhwatzup.net to keep me in her memory and to make sure she wouldn't forget me before the show aired. Well I got what I asked for and more because thirteen days after we met the show finally aired and my boy El Boggie called me up and was like, "Yo China you better call up WBLS fast because Wendy Williams is up there talking about you bad!" I wasn't even heated, I was glad-that's what I wanted her to do! I got on my computer immediately and pulled up the stations contact information and got a hold of Nicole Spence. Nicole was mad cool, she heard me out and told me Wendy Williams wanted to interview me and asked if I was available to go on the air on January 19th at five o'clock, I told Nicole yea and just like that I was booked and another door opened!

Once I found out I was officially a lock as far as the show was concerned I made it a point to attend Wendy's annual Don's and Diva's party at the Canal Room the 18th, one day prior to the show. I was going to make sure I enjoyed myself to the fullest because I knew I wouldn't have much time to hangout after that. Between school, work and being a mother and my new celebrity status I had a lot to contend with. See the difference between me and bitches like Super Head and everybody else is I never got played by none of these niggas, and I was still fucking with some of them when I decided to go public. I could've stayed quite and continued to play the cut and have fun with Flex and Zab if I wanted because they were my main jump off's but where would that get me in the end? Nowhere. Funk Master Flex and Zab Judah are both married so it was never going to be anything more then what it was, and Killa and every other dude in the middle if the industry I fucked with were just dudes I fucked with and nothing more-so fuck it. If I was bold enough to do it, I should be bold enough to own up to it, and at the same time get out of this roller coaster of relationships that I'm in and be financially secure.

I told Flex I was going on The Wendy Williams Experience and planned to go all the way in so he didn't have to hear about it after the fact, because believe me he was going to hear about it. It was no way around it because he's one of the biggest on air personalities in New York City and Wendy's another, not to mention she got fired from Hot 97 in the late nineties and she's been their biggest competition since, so you know she wasn't gonna take it light! It was going down whether Flex liked it or not, he kept asking me, "You got me right … you got me right, you got me?" We played role reversal that night because I didn't say nothing to him this time because he left me no choice. I had to do it because money talks and bullshit walks and Funk Master Flex is fully aware of it and he wasn't trying to come out his pocket so what was I supposed to do? This was my big chance to get broke off and I was fully intent on doing so.

The night of the Don's and Diva party I called Shawn to pick me up and take me to the Canal Room because he's the one with the fat pockets and I also wanted to put it all in his face about how far I have come with this "project" I've been working on. Being that he was totally against me doing the Dr. Keith Ablow Show, but now after he seen what has came out of it, and how my attentions was to get a hold of the world with my story, he would be riding my coat tail, lol. I knew I was playing with fire bringing Shawn to a major event but it was a chance I just had to take, sometimes you gotta go out on limb when you trying to reach the top. I came through getting it crump early! I had some champagne on the house and a few shots of Patron and I aint gonna lie by the end of the night I was finished! Before I could even get settled at the bar a couple of my fans approached me to say hi and show me some love but one of them was out of control, some ghetto bitch grabbed my phone and started trying to save her number in my phone while I was in the middle of sending an important text message! I couldn't believe she was on some star struck shit like that I had to tell her, "Excuse me, you don't just go grabbing my phone like that!" And you know who you are, acting like a damn groupie! Other then that I had fun, Shawn behaved and I even grabbed a couple of girls asses, I don't like girls I just like to flirt. I fucked with Vanessa and Milky at the same time for a little while back in the day but I really didn't see the point in getting my pussy all hot and bothered and tease it with a bootleg dick. To me it just didn't make any sense, I'd rather fuck a man any day.

About an hour and a half after Shawn and I got there I caught a glance of Wendy Williams entering the building and told Shawn I had to get up there because she was in the VIP! And if he was good for nothing before, Shawn was making up for it fast because it turned out that he actually knows Wendy's husband Kevin and went off and talked to whoever he had to and got us in. We had to go through VIP to get through to the other VIP inside of the VIP-it was exclusive like that! When we got settled I made myself at home jumping on couches and acting a fool and enjoying myself and celebrating my success with another bottle of champagne on top of what I already had. It wasn't until the end of the night I saw Zab pop up, he came over and said what up to me and Shawn and then to Wendy and 'nem. I could tell she told him about the Dr. Keith Ablow Show because he looked a little pissed which was true because I later found out at the end of the night Zab was in my baby's father ear begging him to tell me not to mention anything about him and I on Wendy's show the next day.

I thought about what Shawn said the next morning and I love Zab-he's a cool dude, down to earth and real as could be so I decided I wasn't going to mention him. Even though I was blowing up niggas spots left and right, it wasn't nothing personal, it just became a matter of business. If they would've took care of me and hollered at me properly none of what took place would've happened-everything would've still been on the low. They know the consequences of their actions and what it takes to solve them-they chose not to so I went down to The Wendy Williams Experience and did what I had to do. The interview was going good, Wendy asked me a couple of questions to feel me out for example questions like how old am I, what do I do for a living and etc. and then got straight down to business. She got at me but it wasn't nothing I couldn't handle or hadn't expected, everybody knows how Wendy gets down. This was my stage and I was fully prepared for whatever may have occurred because I was determined to shine, so when Wendy asked me about Mr. Judah, I said to myself it's my life and I aint scared of nobody so let's get it poppin! Fuck it!

And boy did I get it poppin, soon as she finished asking me when, where and how it all went down, I heard Zab was on the other line like he wanted a problem! The whole time I'm like okay he wants to embarrass himself on the radio in front of millions because he's going to start lying and I'm going to really shut him the fuck down-so let's do it. The first thing that comes out of Zab's mouth was, "Wendy I would have punched China in the face last night but I wasn't gonna mess up your party!" Bullshit, no one cares about a fucking party if you wanna pop off, who was he kidding, I'm from Brooklyn just like he is, I know the rules. Then this fronting ass nigga has the nerves to tell me, "China you better not come outside and you better stay in the house!" I was thinking to myself, wow I must really be getting to this nigga because his dumb ass is making threats to me while a national audience is listening! I knew I had him and he was just helping my cause so I let him rock. Since I had him in my pocket I told that bitch, "Ooooo I'm scared! Ooooo I'm scared", in the most sarcastic way in order to taunt him into doing something else stupid and then gave him something to think about, "Don't get sued!" You know what the big bad wolf did after that right-he hung up, lol.

Wendy went to a commercial immediately following Zab's ignorant threats and said to me, "China I think you better go because this man is serious and dangerous," maybe she didn't know but I knew, I told her, "I know Zab, he can't do nothing because he will get sued for every last fucking dime he got!" I meant every word and I wish he even tried, that would be the worst move of his career. Since Wendy kept pressing me to leave because there was still that possibility he was serious about fucking me up, I passed Charlamagne my Myspace info to show him messages that Flex left me and bounced. At first I looked at Wendy like I aint running from shit but then I thought about it, I may not have been scared of Zab but he could've at least hurt me or fucked up my face or something crazy like that!

Nicole suggested I wait in the back of the lobby until Vaughn picked me up incase his little dick cheating ass was outside lurking around waiting to catch me slipping. All that hiding and planning was getting on my nerves, I decided from that point from now on any interview I go on I was bringing my burner! Fuck that, he might know how to knock niggas out hard-body but fucking with me he better be able to dodge bullets! I knew going in it could go either way and I accepted that, but I always do what I feel in my heart is right and if that meant putting him on blast-that meant putting him on blast. Zab needs to stop parting all the fucking time and concentrate on winning a fight, in boxing your only as good as your last fight and he's currently on a losing streak so he needs to step his game up and stop worrying about me. His ass is getting too old to be chasing me around and his time is running out so he better focus on the ring and not the club. I can't blame him though ... I'd be getting high and cheating on my wife too if I knew my career was just about over, lol. You know what they say, "more money, more problems, gotta move carefully."

11

Overnight Celebrity

By the end of January I was officially on and it was about to get better, "The Wendy Williams Experience" brought my story to a wider audience and not just the tri-state, I was already the talk of New York so I was really shining! They say if you can make it in New York you can make it anywhere and I made it, I put my time in and then all of a sudden tah-dow I became a celebrity over night. Since I was becoming a problem for a lot of people it was only right Hollywood-T from Drahma Magazine emailed me and told me the CEO of Drahma Magazine, Ray Daniels wanted me to do an interview for their up coming second year anniversary edition.

I ended up meeting Ray and Hollywood-T two weeks later at Vesta Lounge in Manhattan during Ray's birthday party. I was having a ball laughing, partying, drinking and shaking my ass on top of furniture like I normally do. I was also plotting my next move and networking to set up future possibilities to get even more exposure and paper when Shawn wanted to show his ass. I should've known he was going to come out of his cage sooner or later, he was being too good, it was bound to happen sooner or later. It all started when Hollywood-T came over and introduced herself and asked me "who's this guy your with" referring to Shawn. Then without my permission he sticks out his hand like, "Hi I'm China Starr's Manager" and then looks at me like say something and I will embarrass you! I didn't give fuck as usual so I lined him up in front of Hollywood-T for acting out of pocket and told her what it was, "No he's not!" And since he wanted to shoot looks I shot him one back that read "go ahead and fucking play yourself", then Hollywood-T wanted to jump in and instigate shit by looking at Shawn like "I guess she told you."

I buttered Shawn up like a fucking hot pan of farina the way Tatiana loves it to ease the tension and two bottles of Moet later all was forgotten. Shawn's a night time bully but come day time he's softer then Pillsbury Doughboy, I've deal with him long enough to know exactly how to play his card. I already nipped his ideas of management in the butt early, so I wasn't worried about that being an ongoing issue but I made it a point to stress it the next morning incase he thought for a fucking second I was playing. Buying me drinks doesn't equate to management especially when you don't know shit! I put my whole plan together with no assistance from him so what the hell would I need him to manage me for? You know what pissed me off though? Even after Hollywood-T and I showed our ass together and some camera man from "I Party on TV" shot a brief interview with us, T had the fucking nerves to introduce Shawn as my damn manager knowing fully well he wasn't!

I knew I had to watch Hollywood-T after that "manager" stunt she pulled at Vesta's, but after a few weeks of getting the run around from the former managing editor at the magazine Lakena, I knew I had to keep a closer eye on her! Every time that she would call or email me to set an appointment to meet face-to-face something would supposedly happen and she'd end up canceling. I figured after she saw my pictures and got all the dirt on me she could, she was just another crab in the bucket hating on me, so I went above her head and told Ray what the deal was after the third cancellation she pulled. Ray called me up asking why hadn't I done the interview yet because it was getting close to the time he needed to drop his special two-year anniversary dvd/mixtape/magazine edition like it was my fault! After I told him what it was and that I had the feeling Lakena was a hater and he probably needed someone else to do it, she emailed me two days later talking about we'll do a phone interview.

The whole time I'm thinking to myself what was that point of her doing all this scheduling and canceling if we could've just done the shit over the phone to begin with? The shit just didn't make any sense; I don't know why he just couldn't have someone else handle it. When we spoke over the phone she wasn't rude or anything and she got down to the point but towards the end of the record she asked me, "Don't you think people are going to think you're a hoe?" I wasn't surprised she asked me that because she probably thought that herself so I made it a point to make a few things clear and ended our conversation, "People are going to talk regardless so I might as well give them something to talk about, so when they call me a hoe make sure they mention that I am a "paid hoe" while they're at it." Who gives a fuck if people are going think I'm a hoe, do your damn job and write!

I'm telling you the people who work at Drahma is crazy, one Saturday after I could barely get to the phone because I was so hung over Ray calls me at the last minute talking about the photo shoot is today! I don't know what the fuck he was thinking, I told him I'd call him back and went in the bathroom and threw up and took two Tylenol and drunk some ginger ale and got my ass back in the bed like fuck that, lmfao. After I woke up I was still sick as a dog but life goes on and time waits for no one so I got dressed and meet everybody at the W hotel in Manhattan and busted that shit out in two hours, the dvd and photo shoot at the same time! Even on my worst day I'm still more then fuckable so don't get it twisted, you saw me bitches.

    I didn't get a chance to see the pictures or the text of the interview until March 31st at the release party at a spot up in Manhattan, I couldn't wait to see what it looked like but I wasn't that concerned with the flicks because I knew I looked fly-I wanted to see what Lakena actually wrote. Soon as I got the magazine in the club Eb threw her light from her phone against the pages so I could read what it said, I was heated! That bitch put words in my mouth and worded shit to say shit I never even said like, I had sex with a bunch of niggas unprotected-I told her I only had unprotected sex with Zab and Flex and nobody else. I also told her I went to college to make a better life for me and my daughter so I wouldn't have to ask a nigga for shit, but she even fucked that up! She turned that statement into I went to college because of what went down with me and Cuban Lynx, the only part she had on point and made sure she wrote like I said it was, "I'll be a paid hoe."

    I was glad she at least got that right, fucking bitch.

    Not too long after I did the spread for Drahma I was taking a nap cause I was tired as hell the King of gossip and Drahma Ray calls me again while I'm sleeping and asks me would I like to go on the Hot 97 morning show with Miss Jones the next day! I don't know why the fuck he always calls me when I'm trying to catch up on my rest but long as he calls with good news, he can call me anytime. At first I thought I was still dreaming when Ray told me he could get me on the show because it's always been a goal of mine to be on Hot 97 either rapping or singing! But since I didn't have an album dropping Tuesday, I'd just be happy they wanted me on their show to tell my life story and "why not"-that's what Flex always says, lol. I told Ray I was down without a question but I still wasn't sure he was going to be able to pull it off considering Flex works there and has his own show called "Air It Out" and he was already in the magazine and dvd so the secret was out the bag. I don't know what the fuck Ray did but he made it happen, I kept asking him are you serious are you sure you can get me in and Ray was like, "China, I already have, all I need to know is when you want to do it." I'm thinking to myself that's what I'm talking about! I wanted to go on the next morning but it was bad timing so I rescheduled for the following Friday, Ray stay on some last minute shit like it's normal.

During the days leading up to morning show I had too much time to think about what I was going to wear, what I was going to say and what might happen if I became a little nervous. I didn't know if Bobby Trends or Funk Master Flex was going to be there or how they would carry it, you know something is always popping off at Hot 97. Flex might've tried to get on his bullshit and try to punch me in the face like he did Steph Lova before she left and made the power switch. All type of scenarios played out in my head but I wasn't going to let anyone or any possibility stop me from doing what I had to on the morning show. I began to get amped when I thought about how close I was to accomplishing another one of my dreams I told all of my friends and hatters to listen to the radio so they could listen to how I was doing big things public wise.

The night before the show I was restless and just wanted to get the shit over with, anticipation kills me, I just like to go in and do it! I was up early like Ray told me but we ended up running a little late by time him and Craig H. picked me up, but I was cool though, my nerves settled down and I was patiently waiting to make the most of my chance to be on Hot 97. Once I heard Miss Jones mention she had a girl by the name of China Starr coming up to talk about numerous celebrities she's slept with, I was like well at least she got my name right and it was definitely going to be on when I got there! The whole time I'm thinking about how ironic it was that I was about to air Funk Master Flex out on his own station and he has a show by the same name, some things in life are priceless and that was one of them! Who would've ever thought it was about to go down like that between us at his own fucking job, on his own station-Hot 97!?

After we made it past security I made Ray and Craig pray with me for a good show and that we all made it out safe, I must've caught flash backs from toddler dick threatening me on the Wendy Williams show, lol. Before we even went in the studio Miss Jones told Ray she wanted me to go in! First off Miss Jones has some huge mother fucking balls for inviting me to her show knowing I wasn't going to back down and I was about to put at least two of her co-workers on blast and maybe more for all she knew. Michael Shawn the show's producer started hating from the beginning right off top, before I even get in the room he looks me in the eyes and says, "You can't mention Flex's name at any time or we'll cut you off the show." I was like whatever, "Fine, I have enough celeb's to talk about then just Flex's ass", and asked him where my chair was at and left it at that. Of course Michael Shawn sat me next to him, like I gave a fuck, I wasn't going to blow my opportunity for him because he's not worth that much but what's the point if you not trying to go all in, isn't that supposed to be the point of the Hot 97 morning show?

I see they like to go at other people's business all day but when it comes to their own team member they be on the hush-hush tip. What the hell happened to Miss Info at the time? When I was on the show I didn't hear her mention shit about Flex's ass when it was all said and done, and believe me she knew what was going on before any of them: before I did Drahma Magazine and before I did the morning she because we spoke on Myspace. In her email it was "get out of here!" but on air it was only "shout out to Drahma Magazine" to salvage Flex's ass. I don't know why they were being so protective of him anyway when he was trying to get Miss Jones and DJ Envy fired just for having me on the show in the first place.

I didn't let them ruin my mood; I just adjusted my seat to my liking like I do in all interviews and got prepared to do me. Miss Jones started my segment by greeting Ray and then wastes no time getting at me, the first thing she asks me was, "Were you at my birthday party in VIP?" After I told her I was there and Zab invited me up and she was like yeah I remember he was there, and goes on to make a comment about losing her front row seats he promised her to his fight with Cotto my PR King. I don't know if she really wanted them anyway because Cotto whipped the shit outta Zab in that ring and you know I was at home laughing my mother fucking ass off! I'm sure Miss Jones remembered me from her party in November because everybody in VIP heard me yell "get the fuck off me" mad loud cause Zab Juda's perverted little ass snuck up behind me and started straddling and dry humping me! I wasn't trying to draw attention to us but he caught me by surprise and by the time I realized it was him it was too late, everybody looked like what the fuck is going on and saw what he was doing, lol.

Overall the show went well and could've been better if they would've let me mention Flex but I still made it memorable anyway. It was what I thought it was going to be, a bunch of unemployed broke nobodies calling in calling me all types of hoes and shit like I give two fucks. I'm an ex-stripper I've been called worst for less, some dumb ass callers called up talking about, "you're bragging about getting slutted out." Listen who cares as long as long as I'm getting paid you can think what you want to think, there's mad hoes in life, I'm just a paid one. It's like Peavy said in his book, "people talked about me before but now it's called promotion, either way keep doing it."

Plan's executed as far as I'm concerned, money is my main focus and whatever comes in the process let it. There's always going to be people hating and I'll keep using it to my advantage, why should I let people who don't matter affect me? I don't regret anything I did cause I wasn't married and if their cheating on their wives it must not have been much of a fucking marriage at all anyway. And believe me I don't know why Flex was mad at me like this was the first time his wife found out he was a cheating dog! He already had a baby on her with that Spanish Diaz chick, and the funny part about it is my father's last name is Diaz too, I just got my mothers, lol. It sounds like to me Funk Mast Flex sure has a thing for the Diaz family and still hasn't fucking learned not to fuck around with us, lol. I mean really come on, I'm not raping these men, they are the ones calling me all hours of the night and sneaking out the house and in and out of clubs just to get some of this good as pussy. I'm not on a leash-I'm good! I didn't have their home numbers for obvious reasons and I wasn't chasing none of them mother fuckers around or keeping tabs on a single one of them. I couldn't get rid of them niggas if I tried! So what Funk Master Flex is mad at me right now, I bet you if we were in a room right now the last thing we would be doing is arguing-we'd be fucking! Trust me!

I know what I'm talking about and what I'm doing that's why I cursed out damn near every last caller on the morning show hating on me when I was on it. I didn't get at Dr. Keith Ablow when he made comments when I was on his show because there was no need to trip considering he has PHD and has some grounds to talk about what I was doing. But when people call the radio just to be heard and try to stunt on me, hell no I won't take their comments in to consideration. Who are they to be taking seriously like that girl who called up talking about she'd been with celebrities too but that she wasn't going to write a book about it. Okay that's you; maybe you don't have the connections to do it like I do so you can't, but does that make you any better then me? No. The funniest part of it is for a bitch not concerned with writing a book she sure had the nerves to ask Miss Jones what she was doing Saturday because she wanted her to help promote a book for her, and no that bird wasn't being sarcastic because she waited for an answer hoping Jonsey would hold her down. How are you going to talk about me, I hope you're reading this and have figured out ... what I am is a money getter and you are what's considered a groupie aka a broke hoe, see me at my book signing, lmatdb-oh that means "laughing my ass to da bank"!

I couldn't believe the same night when I went to Spy to party with Miss Jones and look at this bullshit this nigga Zab was hating on me like a little bitch! I saw him and Miss Jones chilling together in VIP and decided I'd breeze through to see what was popping and to mingle a little bit. Instead of letting me be and minding his own fucking business or punching me in the face like he said he would, that washed up mother fucker told security don't let me in! I heard all night he was panicking trying to keep tabs on me, and my source wouldn't lie, besides old habits die hard he was always a few steps behind me like my fucking shadow. Who'd ever think a boxer like him would have so many sensitive ways? I didn't even stress not getting in because the real party was downstairs, all the bottles being popped where popped around me because I get any party to jump. As long as China Starr is in the mother fucking building-you good! I swear people started leaving VIP just to get it in with us, lol.

Being the Starr I am I was back on Hot 97 the next morning coming all out of Miss Jones's mouth, it was a bunch of bullshit but it was publicity none the less. She was stunting hard talking about I aint got no pull and I couldn't get in VIP but she never mentioned why. She never said anything about her paranoid ass homeboy-pacing Spy all night with me on his mind, but of course not, why would she? I heard through the grapevine her and Zab have a little history together and I wouldn't be surprised at all, especially since she went out her way to mention my name with lies and just happens to remember me from a party in which we never even spoke. I think she might've got her lil' feelings hurt when she realized the subliminal message Zab was sending by inviting me to VIP at her party and dry humping my ass like a dog in heat that he was not only fucking his wife and her, but anybody else he damn well wanted to. He was just using her for a mouthpiece to promote his fights, lol. She never had nothing bad to say about Mr. Super Zab Juda until he lost to Cotto and even then it was minor like "Zab got the beat down last night", any other time she got a whole lot to say, go figure. Then she turns around and makes an asshole full of racial remarks and slurs about Puerto Rican's, can it be she's just mad her undercover lover can't get enough of Puerto Rican ass-shout out to Hot 97, Miss Jones, DJ Envy and all the morning show listeners! Listen I don't give a fuck what people say about me because the minute they stop that means I'm not on my job, that's when I'll worry, until then tell me how I taste!

12

The Pros and The Cons

I've always been the center of attention throughout my life but now I was dealing with another level of limelight, now it was a necessity to be fresh from head to toe and the streets were always watching. In this game there's no such thing as a time out because you're tired-you gotta go hard or go home every time out because you never what day could be your last. After I received a bunch of criticism for the pictures I took for Alltheparties.com it woke me up and opened my eyes and I started a strict diet immediately! Don't get it fucked up I'm not fat-I'm thick and there's a big difference and I wear it well. I used to be skinny and I can drop weight in a minute so if anything everybody's little comments didn't do anything but help me. If I way fit to a "T" in my pictures from the beginning nobody wouldn't have anything to say other then "hmm" and that would've been that. It just like how everybody talked about how Brittany Spears blew up after the baby but once she got back to dime status everybody jumped right back on her shit! I'm not pressed about my weight at all because I'm using every last one of my haters as my street team promoters and guess what, not a single one of them dumb ass mother fuckers getting a red cent, lol.

The funniest part about the whole situation about me promoting a book called "Celebrities Are Groupies Too" is celeb's still fuck with me! No lie one day I go to check my Myspace messages and I got a message from Craig G. from the Juice Crew talking about, "I want to be in chapters 16, 17 and 18. I read your interview on datzwhatzup.net and I won't have the same problem as Sidekick!" I wasn't familiar with any of Craig's music because he was a little before my time, I'm from the Biggie era, the only back in the day artist I remember by name is Salt-n-Pepper and Whitney Houston. Other then that you'd have to play the song for me, Craig G. did "Symphony" with Cool G. Rap, Big Daddy Kane and Marley Marl and nem so I vaguely recognized his name. I actually didn't give a fuck what songs he did or what he was up to, I was just interested in what he had to say since he was talking about he doesn't have the same problem as Sidekick-I mean Bobby Trends, lol. I basically said Bobby Trends wasn't packing nothing but a IHOP sausage link for a dick and it's true, ask his wife or tell him to show you like Craig G. offered to show me. I didn't have time for games and since Craig G. was contacting me he knew what I was about and what he was getting his self into so I told him "email me a picture."

I figured if Craig was bout it he'd do it because actions speak louder then words and I haven't been properly broke off since Flex fucked me last year, that's the only reason I wish I didn't say nothing about Flex-other then that I could careless, lol. Once I saw how fat and long Craig's dick was I was like "yea I gotta see what he about", I wanted some immediately! After a few days of communicating with each other via email I decided I'd give him a sample of what he wanted to know, what was it about me that had all these celeb's open! I'm sure he figured if he put some work in he could get some publicity for his album coming out because I know after he saw how much publicity his best friend Cool G. Rap got for being Super Head's baby daddy it had to have crossed his mind-I'm not stupid. I was just giving him a chance to fuck me right and if he could, I'd win and if he couldn't he'd loose, simple as that. Besides he looks a little like Young Jeezy and I haven't been able to get to him, so I didn't mind settling for a minor duplicate with a major dick! Yeeeaaa I'm telling you Keyshia you better not let it go, lol.

I was hoping Craig was able to handle all my phat ass and wet pussy because he came to my house in a cab all the way from Yonkers and I didn't want to have to send him back so soon if he couldn't! I knew it was going to be good by looking at it cause it scared me a little, lol, but sometimes you never know. If a nigga don't know what to do with his dick, straight up it's a waste of time of fucking with him. When I opened the door Craig G. already had and L in his mouth smoking! He looked fly in his black blinging Biggie-tee and jeans and I couldn't wait to get it poppin. I wanted him to punish my ass pronto so we went straight to my room and sat on the bed because that's what he was there for, shit we both grown. I didn't have any drawers on because it as no need to for what we was about to do!

I laid on my stomach so he could get a good view of my phat ass and of course it was like a magnet, he started to massage my ass and then rub my clit and it was over! I was wet as hell, lol. The first time he put it in it felt like his dick split the shit out of me, I couldn't even scream! I just took it like a big girl is supposed to, lol, but when that nigga told me to come to the end of the bed for some back shot's, no lie-that shit blew my mother fucking mind!!!! He was stroking the shit out of my ass, all I could hear was my pussy popping and his thighs slapping against my ass, I died and went to good dick heaven. That nigga Craig was a beast with it, he was like the Energizer Bunny, shit he just kept going and going and going and going, I didn't even have to tell him to take all my pussy he already accomplished that, lol. It felt so good when he came all over my ass but it wasn't going to be no fucking round two, my shit was "out of order." He knocked my shit out in one round hard-body, I wish I had a sign to throw up on that mother fucker cause he was damn sure ready for more. I tried to be a big girl and let him beat it up some more but I felt like calling the fucking fire department to cut my pussy off!!!

I was the one who should've been prepared because he told me that he wanted to fuck it up for everybody in every sense of the word and he did just that! I couldn't fuck for two weeks after we first fucked because he ripped my shit up inside and out, after the way he put it down I didn't want to fuck anyone else anyway. Talk about sticking to your word, lol. I mean once you get some good dick you want to keep that last good memory and not fuck it up with a bad one but Flex is still the champion, but the way Craig's been consistently fucking me he's the number one contender.

We still kick it every here and there and right now he's my favorite jump off, Craig's a nice guy and funny as hell, he said to me one day, "Damn you aint even sucking my dick!" I was like, "I'm not Superhead", lol, I could understand where he was coming from because he was giving me quality professional hours of fucking but I'm not famous for sucking dick, I'm famous because I'm a Starr! I think he was halfway serious when he said it but it was probably because he hadn't seen me in awhile and was cranky because he hadn't had any of my magnificent pussy. I know he has feelings for me and I have a little for him but with our lives equally hectic and Shawn always somewhere in the picture it's really not much time to go any further then what it is. That's why I was surprised at how uptight he got when I told him that I had tried out for The Flavor of Love 3. After he said to me, "I'm not going to kiss you after you've kissed Flavor Flav" I thought about it ... he was right! I couldn't kiss that nigga either, lmao. So I decided I can't go through with it and decided to do something else, I figured why not get some more exposure, have some fun in a mansion and fuck up a few loud mouth bitches-I like to fight anyway so it wouldn't be a problem, lol, but I couldn't do it. Flav knows nobody on that show gives two fucks about his ass and that they just want to be on TV but I think that's just one show I'll have to pass on.

Alissa from The Dr. Keith Ablow contacted me about participating in "The MC Serch Project" off the strength of my acting ability and our prior conversation at Fox 5. The MC Serch Project was basically a funkier version of the Tyra

Banks Show NBC was shooting as a pilot to see if Serch would be able to successfully handle his own show. I think Serch did his thing and it was a great experience, I was on a show discussing interracial dating and it was crazy! I was there to discuss why I don't date white men, along with a black guy who didn't date black women and a black girl who didn't agree with black guys dating outside their race but didn't date black guys herself! That would have to be some of the dumbest shit I ever heard, if you believe that then what the fuck are you doing every other race but yours?

Personally it doesn't matter to me who she fucks with because that's her business but I had to say something when she kept making so many contradictory comments and pointless statements. She said her brother was a professional football player and that a lot of white girls from his college were on him like groupies when he was in school, and you know I know first hand it's not always the girls chasing the guy so I told her flat out. I figure he doesn't discriminate, most guys feel pussy's pussy anyway, maybe should try it, she doesn't discriminate against any other race but her own. The point of the show was for us to see a lot of our thoughts of the opposite race are just stereo types and everyone should be judged on a case by case basis, so the show sent us out on a date with the total opposite of who we'd date on our own see we'd see their point.

I didn't mind going on a date with a white guy because I really don't have nothing against them, I just heard on average they got small dicks and you know how I feel about that! You gotta be packing or I aint fuking wit 'cha, and "no" if you wondering, I'm not trying to find out. If I were to date a white guy he'd have to be more to my style of life, you know hip-hop orientated like Emminem, I couldn't fuck with somebody like that character Bret from the Rock of Love, I'd be too much for his ass, lol. Anyway since I had to go on the date I used it to my advantage, I told the guy "we going to kill two birds with one stone" so I told him tell me about his club promotions and I'd discuss my book because I'm always grinding. Needless to say the date went well, I hope the show airs because I had a blast promoting and acting with DJ Co Co Chanel on the ones and twos! Yea the show has its own dj and I was acting my ass off when I told them I had a miraculous change of heart-imagine that, you know I love my big dicks too much for that to go down, lmao. It was a cool. I'd do it again.

You know, even though everybody knows my life from TV, magazines and radio it can be a little annoying when that's all they have to say, like Mel Matrix from the Dipset. I met Mel and Jim Jones at Miss Jones's birthday party last November when Zab was stuck up my ass in VIP, before Jimmy got a chance to get up stairs a fight broke out and him and Mel had to fuck a couple of niggas up.

Some groupie ass nigga got mad because Jim Jones deaded him on an autograph and he started flipping like a female so they beat his ass like a female, I was on the floor rolling! I swear every time I see one of them Byrd Gang niggas they into some shit, luckily me and Mel had a chance to build and he slide me his number to stay in touch before the shit popped off.

Mel is a thug to the death and anybody will tell you that nigga is a certified gangsta because his name rings bells loud in the streets. Me and Mel always had a good vibe but I didn't feel like talking about other niggas when I was at his moms house in Brooklyn. He kept asking me questions about Flex because he said he didn't like him because he be dick sucking niggas, like one minute he playing Jimmy close the next minute he's playing True Life close like he just couldn't make up his mind whose dick he wanted to suck, lol. If you listen to Hot 97 you know what he's talking about. When we started talking about the shows I did he told me he didn't agree with it and was like, "that's like sitting in front of the judge", ask me did I give a fuck. I mean I respect Mel Matrix because he's a real ass nigga and I understood the angle he was coming from. But you know how I play, I told you before money talks and bullshit walks, you learn that in Hustling 101 and everybody's hustling. That mother fucker Vaughn tried to play me!

I peeped Vaughn's hand early so I gave him enough room to hang himself and canceled his ass early. One night we got into an argument when he was drunk because he called me talking about "what's up it's your manager", my mana-who? I pulled the phone away from my ear and looked at it like I know this mother fucker didn't just sit her and say he's my manager! He had to be doing more then drinking to say some shit like that so I said to him, "What the fuck do you know about managing? You didn't help me write my book, you didn't book none of my shows, you didn't help me get on any of the radio stations I was on-you didn't do shit but take pictures!" He told me I was fucked up for saying that but I was like "naugh you fucked up", nobody told him to try to make his position more then what is was, from that point on all he could ever do was take pictures.

Vaughn actually tried to reason with me to let him be my manager by stating that there are plenty of people who are made managers that don't know shit about managing. Duh, but what the fuck would I want a manager that doesn't know shit? I told him I need someone connected and capable of getting me spots like Hot 97 and asked him could he do that and then he shut the fuck up, because he knew he couldn't, lol. Ray wasn't my manager but I said that to prove my point so he could cry a river build a boat and get over it. I'm my own boss and I have contacts and male groupies across the globe so what I look like sitting under a nigga while he gets rich off of me? Far as I'm concerned Vaughn is finished, Craig G already ran his spot of jump off so he could go about his business, if he ever gets his shit straight maybe I'll let him come see me. Until then, whatever, I'm tired of telling niggas I do this shit and I'm good at it, you know my fucking name don't you? Alright then.

13

"The Prelude"

I'll be graduating this coming June with an associate degree and enrolling in a program to receive my bachelor and master degree in human and child development? I want to further help victims of domestic violence because I believe life is much more then learning from your mistakes but also contributing to society. I pray to be in the position to some day help people achieve happiness and independence as the shelter has done for me. With God's blessings I plan on establishing a non-profit organization of my own for battered women across the globe. After going through all that I've been through its become a dream of mine to touch the lives of victims of abuse abroad as well as within the United States just the same. Abuse in any form is not tolerable nor does it have a limit or preference to his it effects, it's wrong in any case and needs to stop.

I firmly believe I've gone through my struggle for a reason and the release of my life story is only the beginning of my quest to make the world a better place for others to live in, well at least as much as possible. I believe God has prepared me for bigger things in life and I fully intend on materializing his plan to educate, assist and heal others through my life experiences. If only one female or male leaves an abusive relationship or gains the courage and strength to walk away from an abusive situation, all the time and energy put into the creation of this book was worth it!

China Starr

978-0-595-47845-3
0-595-47845-X